WHAT PEO
SAYING ABC

Thank you, Joachim. I found this book insightful, provocative, and scholarly. You have obviously done your homework. You opened my eyes, challenged my presupposition, and transformed my understanding. Because of the work you have done, I have a greater appreciation for the sovereignty and the grace of God than I've ever had before.

—Bishop Darlingston Johnson.
Bethel World Outreach Ministries
Silver Spring, Maryland.

Elder Joachim Acolatse's love for the Word of God has led him to develop a passion to "Study to show thyself approved unto God…" This has ignited a burning desire in him to search for and discover the truths of God's Word. In this pursuit, God has revealed himself to Elder Acolatse through his Word under the supervision of the Holy Spirit. The elder shares these revelations here. As you advance through the pages of this book the truth unfolds, breaking the shackles and chains of ignorance and setting you free—free indeed.

—Reverend Michael Macauley.
Nation of Christ Church
Georgia.

An inspirational book on the life of Samson that will challenge traditional views concerning this man of faith.

—Kimberly M. Scott

SAMSON

SAMSON

GOD'S MIGHTY MAN OF FAITH

JOACHIM ACOLATSE

TATE PUBLISHING *& Enterprises*

Published by Tate Publishing & Enterprises, LLC
127 E. Trade Center Terrace | Mustang, Oklahoma 73064 USA
1.888.361.9473 | www.tatepublishing.com

Tate Publishing is committed to excellence in the publishing industry. The company reflects the philosophy established by the founders, based on Psalm 68:11,
"The Lord gave the word and great was the company of those who published it."

Book design copyright © 2010 by Tate Publishing, LLC. All rights reserved.
Cover design by Amber Gulilat
Interior design by Chris Webb

Published in the United States of America

ISBN: 978-1-61663-198-7
Religion / Biblical Biography / Old Testament
10.02.17

Dedication

This work is dedicated to all crusaders for righteousness and to the spirit of the Nazarite in the believer whose burning desire is to overspread the earth with the kingdom of righteousness: Your every thought is permeated with righteousness; your every word promotes righteousness; your every deed establishes righteousness.

Therefore, O man, you are a fearer of God; a hater of evil. The Spirit of the Lion of the tribe of Y'hudah (Judah) indwells you. You, therefore, will not turn away from confronting evil. Victory is yours always, for you are empowered to overcome the world by your faith and to redeem the times, for the day is evil.

Let righteousness be spread abroad through you. Let righteousness be spread, if only, by you. Let righteousness reign!

Sanctify yourself, now, unto the Lord that you should be consecrated by his Holy Spirit.

ACKNOWLEDGMENTS

Many thanks and love to the Lord for his grace to instill within me the spirit of knowledge, understanding, and wisdom, which made this work possible; to Bishop Darlingston Johnson for his unrelenting questioning that led to the inclusion of the subtitle "Under Appeal;" to my former pastor, Magnus Koker-Thomas, for his incisive review and encouragement to make this work more than an exercise of enlightenment, and also a call to evangelism of the Jew first, then the Gentile; and finally, to Reverend Michael Macauley, my brother in-law, for his review and editing of the final draft. Many thanks for their financial assistance to members of my family—my sister, Barbara, brother, James, and Khadizeth, my niece—without whom this work would not be published in book form at this time. You are the embodiment of the old Liberian proverb, "If house don't sell, street won't buy." Khadizeth, thanks for the enthusiastic discussions—they were very uplifting. May the Lord reward each one of you richly. Amen.

TABLE OF CONTENTS

PREFACE

> All Scripture is given by inspiration of God, and is profitable for doctrine, for reproof, for correction, for instruction in righteousness: That the man of God may be perfect, thoroughly furnished unto all good works.
>
> 2 Timothy 3:16

The chronicle of Shimshon's (Samson's) life on earth during the period of the judges of Israel has confounded the religious community throughout the ages. The clergy, especially, do not know how to handle such a hot potato. Surely God did not condone his servant committing acts of fornication in order to accomplish the divine will. To them, that's blasphemy! So they bellow from the pulpits against a man who was greatly anointed of God but failed to accomplish his mission because he could not master the lusts of his flesh. And they warn us not to be like Shimshon (Samson).

But nothing could be further from the truth, and it is precisely against this gross undermining of God's Word that this book is written. Christians are being robbed of faith, love, and power today by the very same shepherds who are charged to "feed my sheep." On the other hand, there are numerous sincere, hard-working, and dedicated clergymen who are pressing on toward the mark for the prize of the high calling of God in Messiah. This criticism is not leveled at you. Even as a "curse causeless will not alight upon you," so generalized criticism of the clergy will have no effect upon the true servant of God. Be not discouraged, but continue in sound doctrine, ministering to the needs of the sheepfold.

Nearly two thousand years since the Lord dwelled among men on earth, disseminating the truths of the kingdom, the church leadership-pastors, teachers, and preachers-is still hard pressed to feed his sheep the meat of God's Word. Thus, we find the body of Christ is anemic, weak, and unable to fulfill the "greater works" of its calling. Must the condition of the Lord's body on earth continue on this path? How can the anemia be remedied? Have those who don Kefa's (Peter's) mantle neglected, first, to strengthen themselves in the Lord before setting out to tend his sheep? Yeshua (Jesus) cautioned Kefa (Peter), "...When thou art converted, strengthen thy brethren," for if you love me, you will "Feed my sheep" (Luke 22:32; John 21:17). Unfortunately, those who have taken up Kefa's (Peter's) mantle are so busy maligning him to the sheepfold and exalting themselves in the process that the sheep go unfed. Truthfully, not one of these is worthy to untie Kefa's (Peter's) shoelace. Though the Word of God instructs them to "Study to shew thyself approved unto God..." these, self-proclaimed superiors to Kefa (Peter), sermonize to show themselves approved unto men; busybodies who invariably fall into sin, violating the Word of God (2 Timothy 2:15).

And so it goes, from denomination to denomination, from one Sunday to the next, that unwholesome sermons are preached from pulpit to pulpit. In the words of the late Leonard Ravenhill, "The tragedy of this late hour is that we have too many dead men in the pulpits giving out too many dead sermons to too many dead people."[1] The Church needs to be revived!

In the past, I listened with chagrin as a minister of the gospel used up precious time lambasting Shimshon (Samson) in a series which he entitled "Four Bad Boys of Faith" (a misnomer since people of faith cannot be bad). Shimshon (Samson) was portrayed as the only man blessed with super-human strength called to carry out God's plan, but he failed God due to his many vices. So why didn't God remove his anointing from upon Shimshon (Samson)? Another minister cautioned his listeners not to be unrepentant as Shimshon (Samson). God, he said, continued to work through Shimshon (Samson) only because God's message can neither be affected nor changed by the messenger. Does this mean that God's plan can be held captive by mere dispensable man?

Such faithless and contradictory teachings only tend to rob the body of believers of their faith because faith is gained by hearing the Word of God. Is it any wonder then, that today's Christians are anemic and devoid of faith in God after hearing an entire hour of words contrary to the Word of God? It is very important that all believers in Yeshua ha Mashiach (Jesus the Christ) are equally fed the same spiritual diet in order for them to mature and become thoroughly equipped for the glory of God on earth.

Whose report, then, will you believe: God's or the preachers'? God speaks highly of Shimshon (Samson), calling him a notable man of faith, an overcomer. If the preachers tell you, their captive audiences, that Shimshon (Samson) was a failure and God steadfastly calls him a man of faith, who do you believe? Yet, we have endured this argument for three millennia, navigating between "couldn't be" and "yeah, but," while uncomfortably clinging to the fact that God cannot lie! Isn't it about time that we stopped vacillating between the two?

I believe that by the time you read through the last word of this book, you will be convinced that Shimshon (Samson), indeed, was a mighty man of faith who was unfailing in obedience to the divine will to advance salvation beyond the beachhead of the promised land and throughout the earth. Furthermore, I hope to stir up and awaken the Spirit-controlled fire of the Nazarite in you—that by the consecration of the Lord upon you, righteousness will advance from flickering dots of light to brilliant panoramic beams illuminating the earth.

This book introduces, or opens, but does not fully develop or close many theological topics. If fully developed, then this work would be rather voluminous and detract from the object of this study, Shimshon (Samson), the deliverer. Instead, it is hoped that many virtuous discussions will emanate out of this work to the end that the body of Messiah will be edified.

After you have read this book, please open your Bible and begin a worthwhile study into the life of this man, and allow the living Word of God to distill through your mind and into your heart.

Amen.

PROLOGUE

The body of Yeshua ha Mashiach (Jesus the Christ) in the earth today needs to come into the full revelation of the mystery surrounding the mission and events in the life of Shimshon (Samson), God's faithful servant. Such understanding is crucial in building faith in the body and advancing the kingdom of God in the earth. It is also useful in exposing how subtle the devil is as he sows seeds of disunity, thereby keeping the kingdom mired in internal conflict for ages. As the people of God were delivered out of bondage in Egypt and ushered into a land flowing with milk and honey, so are we delivered from the wages of sin into the eternal grace of our Lord today. Nonetheless, the early Church of God languished for centuries in the promised land because they repeatedly transgressed God's law, thereby bringing judgment upon themselves. That is, until the arrival of Shimshon (Samson), the deliverer.

Similarly, the present day Church of Yeshua ha Mashiach (Jesus the Christ) has sputtered along its own way despite being empowered by him to "occupy until I return," and has failed to accomplish the "greater works" he so assuredly told us we would do in his absence.

Failure of the first Church in the promised land to advance God's kingdom in the earth was caused by lack of love, disunity, and pride; every man did what was right in his own eyes. Failure of the present-day Church to advance God's kingdom in the earth is caused, again, by lack of love, disunity, and pride.

The "Great Commission" that the Church so proudly boasts it upholds, states, "Go therefore and make disciples of all nations, beginning from Jerusalem, baptizing them in the name of the Father and of the Son and of the Holy Spirit, and teaching them to obey everything that I have commanded you. And remember, I am with you always, to the end of the age." (Matthew 28:19–20 and Luke 24:47; Revised Standard Version, my arrangement).

Despite the Church's boast of taking the good news into all the world, that so-called "taking" is at variance with two tenets of the command: First, to make disciples of all nations, and second, to begin at Jerusalem. The Church has set about its busy task of making believers in some nations. Wherever preaching the gospel is safe, where there is no opposition or threat to life, the Church will be found. Where the prospects for financial gain are good, there the Church proliferates. The Church has also stopped short at making converts but not disciples. It does not consider that the making of believers is merely part one of the process of making disciples. Without disciples, the greater works cannot be accomplished, as has been seen in the Church's annals since the passing on of the first-century Church. Consequently, we see the absence of agape and the increase of pride and disunity by the proliferation of denominations. Additionally, realizing the impracticality of so many denominations setting up churches in Jerusalem, the Church just simply left off "beginning at Jerusalem."

On the day of Pentecost, over three thousand souls

listened in Jerusalem to the good news, preached and explained to each in his own tongue. Those believing souls then returned to their countries of residence equipped to disseminate the good news also. Flames from the torches lit at Pentecost spread like wildfire around the world until the evil one succeeded in dividing the gentile believer from the Jewish believer. So began the dark ages.

Through pride, gentile Christians endued with the power of the Holy Ghost decided that they no longer needed Jewish leadership. As a result, the Church has become predominantly gentile and has overturned and opposed the influence of Jewish culture and tradition upon the gospel. Therefore, gentile Christians have inherited a gospel that is increasingly painted in black and white with respect to interpretation and understanding. Only through restoration of the Jewish brotherhood will the Church again be equipped in love with the full living color of the gospel, fully capable of accomplishing the "greater works" as the first-century Church did.

In order to pay due respect to the Jewishness of Scripture, references to the Lord, for example, will be by his Jewish name, Yeshua, followed initially by the gentile equivalent, Jesus, in parentheses, such as Yeshua ha Mashiach (Jesus the Christ/Messiah) or Shimshon (Samson). The dual reference will be dropped later when you have become accustomed to the Jewish appellation. The idea is that if we, Christians, begin to honor our Jewish roots, evangelical gaps between Jew and gentile might be bridged. Let each of us, therefore, spare no effort to reach out in love to one Jewish soul; for we owe them much. As it is written, "Have they stumbled that they should fall? God forbid: but rather through their fall salvation is come unto the Gentiles, for to provoke them to jealousy ... for salvation is of the Jews" (Romans 11:11; John 4:22).

Pray that the Church will learn that love is to obey the entire Word of God. By knowing this, we will begin to love one another, and the world will know that we are one in Yeshua (Jesus).

Finally, a word of fairness: criticism leveled against the church, clergy, and congregation is intended to be constructive. I dare not let this work become a divisive element in the hands of Satan against the Church of God. There are many very dedicated, diligent clergymen who are doing the work of the Lord today. There are also very many publicized and unpublicized martyrs who have given their lives for the gospel of Yeshua ha Mashiach (Jesus the Christ) today. This is not the platform upon which your accolades are proclaimed. Instead, one day, the Master will welcome you into his kingdom in heaven and proclaim, "Well done, thou good and faithful servant" (Matthew 25:21). Until then, it is hoped that the body of Mashiach will be spurred on to greater works, rooted and grounded in the Lord and in the power of his might, not giving ground to Satan and his uncircumcised evil band, but redeeming the times through strength in love and the testimonies of his Word. Amen!

The Allegations
Against Samson

The life story of Shimshon (Samson) has been an enigma to his contemporaries, as well as to the people of God throughout the ages. Shimshon's biography, as given by inspiration of God, contains more than ample information to show forth the coming saving work of Mashiach. In more complete terms, Shimshon was a precursor of Yeshua ha Mashiach (Jesus the Christ).

Even as the omnipotent God, in the frailty of human flesh, died in order to accomplish his task, so did Shimshon. These two historic figures are still a stumbling block in the first instance and an enigma in the second instance to the Jew. The block of stumbling to the Jew was the doorway for the Gentiles unto salvation. On the other hand, Shimshon's case has been a dilemma both to Jew and Gentile because his mission seemingly ended in failure—short-circuited before it could be accomplished—despite the tremendous outpouring of God's grace and might upon him.

Jew and Gentile alike conclude that Shimshon failed

to accomplish his mission largely because he succumbed to his own lusts. Yet they are at a loss to explain why God, in all his holiness, would continue to work through such a sinful man. Here are tidbits of what they have to say, beginning with their allegations.

> There are essentially three conditions which constitute the Nazarite vow[2]:
> - Eat nothing from the vine, neither drink wine nor strong drink.
> - Do not make contact with any dead thing, and
> - Put no razor to the hair of your head.

Shimshon, a Nazarite, is alleged to have broken two of these conditions while having the third imposed on him due to his own weakness. A fourth allegation, though not part of the Nazarite vow, is levied against him because he married outside of his own people. In addition, it is alleged that he openly committed fornication, and finally, that he failed God by not fulfilling his mission.

Charge number one: A Nazarite is forbidden to drink wine or strong drink, or to eat anything from the vine. The defendant, Shimshon, did indeed imbibe.

Charge number two: A Nazarite is forbidden to eat any unclean thing. The defendant took and ate honey from the carcass of a lion.

Charge number three: A Nazarite is forbidden from touching any dead thing. The defendant slew a lion and many Philistines with his bare hands, thereby making contact with the dead.

Charge number four: The Nazarite must not allow a razor to come upon his head. The defendant revealed this secret to his enemies, thereby aiding the enemy.

Charge number five: The Israelite is commanded never to intermarry with the uncircumcised people who lived in the Promised Land. The defendant took a wife from among the heathen people.

Charge number six: It is commanded that "Thou shalt not commit adultery." The defendant actively engaged in sexual activity outside of marriage.

Charge number seven: Through his own lust, Shimshon failed to accomplish the task that the Lord gave him.

A Defensible Case

One might argue, and rightly so, that the book of Judges informs us that during the period of the judges of Israel, everyone did what was right in his own sight. So it is commonly thought that Shimshon also did likewise. Therein lies the error because Shimshon was meticulously unpresumptuous in his relationship with God.

If Shimshon were brought before an assembly of today's clerics to answer the charges levied against him, he, doubtless, would be found guilty. The preponderance of fact, fiction, and circumstantial evidence against him seem overwhelming. At least that's the way it seems. However, this is not an open and shut case that is weighted heavily in favor of his accusers. In fact, the Holy Spirit would be only too glad to lead the defense of Shimshon, his servant.

It is important to note that Shimshon's contemporaries did not levy any charges against him. If they did, Scripture is silent. On the contrary, he is a noted elder of faith in the same company as Shmu'el (Samuel), Moshe (Moses), David, Y'hoshua (Joshua), and so on.[3] It would appear that Scripture contains some information that we have not deciphered yet.

A word of caution: Until the religious community can

ascertain exactly what mission was given for Shimshon to accomplish, let all take heed, and "accuse not a servant unto his master, lest he curse thee, and thou be found guilty" (Proverbs 30:10). How else can one evaluate the work of another without first knowing the objective of his mission? Nevertheless, it would be profitable for us to discover what others have said in order that we may be able to correct them after we have ourselves been corrected.

What Do Others Say?
Halley's Bible Handbook

A short treatment is accorded the history of Samson in the twenty-fifth edition of Halley's Bible Handbook. In it, it is reported that Samson, a Danite, was appointed by God before his birth to deliver Israel from the Philistines. Endowed with superhuman strength, he wrought some amazing feats. Unfortunately, this was a man who knew personal weakness and tragedy. It is mentioned that his weakness was turned into strength, which account can be found in the commentary on the heroes of faith in the book of Hebrews. He is the last named judge of record in the book of Judges.[4]

Josephus

Josephus, the noted Jewish historian, gives a lengthy and engaging account of Samson's history that runs almost parallel to Scripture. Beginning at the divine announcement of his coming birth and continuing to his tragic death, Josephus mixes truths embellished with part truths, even going into the mind of Samson on occasion. However, to his credit, his report is based on second or third parties at best, since he was not contemporary with Samson.

To begin, he tells us of a man, Manoah, of great virtue who was a prominent person among his countrymen; and his wife, a woman celebrated for her beauty far above her contemporaries. The Lord hearkened to the entreaty of this couple to give them offspring from their own bodies.

In response, a strikingly handsome angel of the Lord appeared, at a time when the husband was absent, to foretell the birth, mission, and destiny of a son soon to be born to them. Upon his return, the wife related the event, not leaving out the perceived handsomeness of the young man. Her husband soon became rather jealous and suspicious toward her. Therefore, the woman entreated the Lord to again dispatch the angel for her husband's benefit, and thereby relieve her from the heightened state of excitement brought on by his passion. So once again, the angel appeared to the woman. This time, the wife requested him to stay put until she fetched her husband. Still under suspicion, Manoah arrived and engaged the angel in conversation to ascertain who he was and how they were to raise up the child. Having heard the good news with his own ears and seen the angel perform wonderfully in their sight, Manoah was filled with trepidation due to fear that they had seen God.

In due time, the woman gave birth to a son whom they named Samson, which name signifies "one who is strong." Now, the angel had enjoined the woman and her husband that this son would be a goodly child of great strength who would afflict the Philistines when he became a man. Therefore, his hair should not be cut, nor should he drink anything other than water.

Eventually, Samson grew up and fell in love with a Philistine maiden of Timnath, whom he would marry. Although his parents objected to his desire (for she was not an Israelite), they finally relented and proceeded to procure her for his wife. During the espousal period on his way to visit her, he encountered and killed a lion. After some time and during another one of his visits, he discovered that bees were making honey in the carcass of the lion. Breaking off three honeycombs, he gave them among his presents to his espoused.

As was customary, Samson hosted the wedding feast over a seven-day period. The Philistines, out of fear of his strength, assigned thirty of their strongest young men to be his companions. During the merry-making, Samson propounded a riddle to his companions. He promised to present each one with a shirt and a garment if they could discover the answer to his riddle by the seventh day. The consequence of failure on their part would be a present to him of a shirt and garment from each one of them.

Not being able to discover it by the third day, and knowing time was running out, the young men then enjoined Samson's bride to discover the answer from her husband and reveal it to them, or else they would burn her and her family. Thereupon, she set out to deceive him and revealed the secret to his companions soon after it had been confided to her. To this treachery, Samson replied, "Nothing is more deceitful than a woman; for such was the person that discovered my interpretation to you."

Keeping true to his promise, he gave each of his companions accordingly, taking spoils from thirty Philistines of Ashkelon who became his prey. But in a spate of anger, he divorced his wife. In turn, she, despising his anger, was married to the companion who had made the match between them previously.

Reacting to this injurious treatment, Samson resolved to take vengeance upon both his wife and the Philistines. He thus captured three hundred foxes, tied lighted torches to their tails, and released them in tandem into their grain fields, which were already ripe for harvest. This resulted in the total destruction of their food crops and prompted an investigation into who had committed the act and why.

Discovering that Samson was the responsible party and that he had just cause, the Philistines exacted punishment upon Samson's wife and her family by burning them with fire. Samson, in turn, took revenge upon the Philistines for his wife. After slaying many of them, he began to dwell at Etam, a strong rock of the tribe of Judah.

So the Philistines made an expedition against that tribe on account of Samson's deeds against them. But the people of Judah argued that they were being unfairly targeted because of Samson. Therefore, the Philistines agreed not to war against them if they would deliver Samson into their power. At Samson's concurrence, they bound and delivered him to the Philistines, who for the joy of having under their power one who had inflicted great destruction upon them, came upon him with shouting. But Samson broke his bonds, picked up the jawbone of an ass that lay nearby, and with it, smote and slew a thousand warriors. The rest of them fled in great disorder.

Now Samson was filled with pride at such a great exploit, whereby he proclaimed that it came about by his own proclivity and the dread his enemies had of him. Thereupon, a great thirst came over him so that he soon reasoned that human courage was nothing and ascribed it all to God instead. He then repented, asking God to help him and not let him fall into the hands of his enemies. Mercifully, God, being moved by his entreaties, provided a bountiful supply of sweet water from a certain rock. And Samson called the site "Jawbone," as it is today.

Now holding the Philistines in contempt, Samson openly took up lodging in a certain inn in Gaza. The leaders, thus being informed, set up watch at the gates of the city with men in ambush to prevent his escape. But being acquainted with their plans, Samson rose about midnight and ran upon the gates with force, lifting and removing them, along with their posts, beams, and wooden furniture. He then bore them away past Hebron, where he deposited them.

Continuing in his own way and adopting the customs of the Philistines, Samson transgressed the laws of Israel, thereby initiating his own miseries. He fell in love and began to live with a Philistine woman who was a harlot. Her name was Delilah. The Lords of the Philistines soon induced her with money to discover the source of Samson's great and invincible strength. Taking advantage of an occasion as they were drinking, Delilah sought to learn the secret of Samson's superhuman strength. However, not yet having lost his senses, he managed to elude her subtlety for a while. Nevertheless, under her constant barrage, he finally gave up and revealed the origin of his great strength; thereby were the Philistines able to subdue and imprison Samson.

During one of their public festivals, when all the rulers and prominent people gathered under one roof to celebrate, they sent for and put Samson in their midst, where he could receive heaps upon heaps of insults as they toasted their success. Samson, whose hair had since grown long again, imagined how he could exact revenge upon his enemies for such great insults. Under the guise that he was weary, he persuaded the boy that led him by the hand to bring him near the pillars, for he desired rest. As soon as he neared them, he rushed with force and brought the building down, slaying three thousand men in addition to himself.

So ended the life of this man who had ruled over the Israelites for twenty years. Nevertheless, this was an extraordinary man who deserves to be admired for his "courage, strength, and magnanimity. Besides the fact that by human nature he proved too weak to resist the wiles of a woman, in every other respect, testimony is given that Samson was a man of extraordinary virtue."[5]

The Jewish Encyclopedia

The Jewish Encyclopedia gives a very good account of Samson's history, which is, in my opinion, succinct and more incisive than Josephus's. The last paragraph of the article is noteworthy to be paraphrased here.

Chapter sixteen of the book of Judges records the disgraceful and disastrous end of Samson. He was profoundly fascinated by Philistine women. Note the similar strategy used first by his wife, and then by Delilah to extract his secrets and betray him to his enemies. Samson's was a life filled with tragedy. His heroic deeds, notwithstanding, did not release Israel from oppression of the Philistines.

A supplementary section culled from rabbinical sources gives some interesting information not found in the biblical accounts. He is identified as Bedan or Ben Dan, a descendant of the tribe of Dan. His mother is identified as a woman of the tribe of Judah whose name was Zeleponit or Hazeleponit. The name Samson is derived from the Hebrew shemesh, meaning "sun." By association with Psalm 84:11, Samson bore the name of God who is a "sun and shield." Even as God is a protector of Israel, so did Samson watch over Israel in his time. In another respect, he resembled God in never needing aid or help.

Samson was the object in mind when Jacob pronounced the blessings upon Dan: (1) likening him to the Messiah,

(2) likening him to a serpent since his power rested in his head (i.e. .... hair) and because he was revengeful, lived solitarily, and slew more of his enemies at his death than during his lifetime even as the serpent's venom continues to kill after it is dead.

Throughout his judgeship, it is pointed out that Samson never needed any service from any Israelite and piously observed not to take the name of the Lord in vain. When he pulled down the temple of Dagon, thereby slaying more than three thousand Philistines and himself, the structure toppled backward so that his body was preserved and uncrushed, for his family to find and bury.[6]

Secular World: BBC News Report (February 15, 2001)

A BBC news article quoting from the New Scientist, reports that Dr. Eric Altschuler of the University of California in San Diego claims that Samson, instead of being a hero, was mentally ill and a thug. According to Dr. Altschuler, who characterizes Samson as one having an anti-social personality disorder (ASPD), people diagnosed with ASPD exhibit at least three of seven specific behavioral traits: Samson is diagnosed as exhibiting six of the seven traits.[7]

Conclusion

Generally, the consensus on Shimshon (Samson) is not favorable. The secular world declares him to be a bully while the Judeo-Christian community warns those within the ranks not to be like Shimshon (Samson). A noted multi-media Bible teacher is on record as saying that the truth of the message of God does not depend on the messenger. He portrays Shimshon (Samson) as one anointed of God who went astray, yet he continued to function under the anointing of God. Still another warns men not to fall to the "Samson Syndrome." And do not forget the "Bad Boy of Faith" appellation—which makes one to wonder how God could have made the mistake of including Shimshon (Samson) among the notable elders of faith.

The Biblical Account

You have read a brief but comprehensive report of how the secular as well as the religious communities view Shimshon (Samson). As we navigate the biblical accounts of his life, it is rather important that everyone is shorn of all prior conceptions that would hinder the truth of God's Word entering in. Without doubt, there is major discrepancy between what Scripture says and what others tell us concerning Shimshon. You also ought to judge for yourself between what others say and what Scripture says.

Scripture proclaims him to be a notable elder of faith who obtained a good report through faith, "For by it [faith] the elders obtained a good report. And what shall I more say? For the time would fail me to tell of Gedeon, and of Barak, and of Samson, and of Jephthae; of David also, and Samuel, and of the prophets ... And these all, having obtained a good report through faith, received not the promise" (Hebrews 11:2, 32, 39). In spite of this, the religious community proclaims that Shimshon failed God. Perhaps what they really mean is that he failed to conduct his life according to how they would have liked him to.

Since Shimshon received a good report, then he indeed is a man of faith, of whom the Master has said, "Well done, thou good and faithful servant: thou hast been faithful over a few things, I will make thee ruler over many things: enter thou into the joy of thy Lord" (Matthew 25:21). The mystery that must be unraveled is in what or over what was Shimshon faithful.

Sheep without a Shepherd

After Joshua and all of that generation who knew the Lord died, there arose another generation in the promised land who did not know the Lord, nor the exploits that he had done for Israel. Then the children of Israel forsook the Lord, the God of their fathers, and began to worship the gods of the people who lived in their midst. Therefore, God's anger was kindled against them. Consequently, he allowed the people who dwelled among them to rule over and oppress them.[8]

Nevertheless, because of his mercy toward them, God hearkened to the voice of their groanings under the yoke of their enemies and delivered them. Time after time, God raised up judges through whom he worked to deliver Israel. However, just as often as he did, Israel forsook the Lord and worshiped other gods. It happened that whenever the judge died, Israel turned back to doing exactly what had put them under subjection of their enemies. This was a case of sheep without a shepherd: A fragmented nation that needed to be galvanized under one leader with one common goal and purpose.

So it was that after the death of Abdon, the thirteenth judge of Israel, the children of Israel again did what was evil in the sight of God. This time, the Lord delivered them under the yoke of the Philistines.

The Philistines have their beginnings in Ham, one of Noah's three sons. Ham was the father of Cush, Mizraim, Phut, and Canaan. Mizraim fathered seven sons, one of whom, Casluhim, was the father of Philistim. From Philistim come the Philistines, seafarers who settled the coastal valleys and plains of the land (which was later promised to Abram) among their cousins, the Canaanites (Sidonians, Jebusites, Amorites, Girgasites, and Hivites, among others). The children of Israel descended from Shem, Ham's brother. They were fated to be the antagonists of the Canaanites because of the curse pronounced upon Canaan by Noah, his grandfather.

Unbeknownst to the children of Israel, the Lord had simultaneously begun to prepare a deliverer for them— one who would usher in the next phase of the salvation of his people. For Israel (Jacob) had wistfully prophesied, "I have waited for thy salvation, O Lord" (Genesis 49:18).

A Son Shall Be Born

To the Danite, Manoah, and his wife, an angel was sent from the Lord with the astounding news of the coming birth of a special son. Not only were there divine restrictions on the life of this child, the mother was also required to exercise certain restrictions in her life. Apparently, while she was with child and until the child was weaned, the mother was required to abstain from drinking wine or strong drink, from eating anything derived from the grapevine, and from eating any unclean thing.

The angel of the Lord that appeared unto the woman had said: "Behold now, thou art barren, and bearest not: but thou shalt conceive and bear a son. Now therefore beware, I pray thee, and drink not wine nor strong drink, and eat not any unclean thing: For, lo, thou shalt conceive, and bear a son; and no razor shall come on his head; for the child shall be a Nazarite unto God from the womb: and he shall begin to deliver Israel out of the hand of the Philistines" (Judges 13:3–5).

Implicit in this message is that only by divine intervention would the woman conceive a child. And conditional to the divine intervention is her unconditional obedience to the instruction: ingest no wine, strong drink, or unclean thing for the Lord, your God, has ordained this child to be a Nazarite unto himself, and no razor shall come upon his head.

Upon hearing this, Manoah, the father desired a re-visitation by the angel of the Lord to teach them how the child should be trained up. In response to his entreaty, the angel of the Lord was dispatched to reiterate to both of them, "All that I commanded her, let her observe" (Judges 13:14). It was therefore the parents' responsibility to train the child to live in obedience to his calling. In due time, he would begin to deliver Israel from under the oppression of their enemy.

It came to pass that the woman bore a son whom she named Shimshon (derived from shemesh, which means bright, brilliant, sun). The favor of the Lord was upon the child as he grew. Beginning in the land area allotted to the tribe of Dan between Zorah and Eshtaol, the Spirit of the Lord began to *move* him. When he came of age, Shimshon fell in love with a Philistine woman of the city of Timnath. Returning from a visit there, he successfully lobbied his parents, over their objections, to make the necessary marital arrangements so that she would become his bride. It was not apparent to the parents that Shimshon's desire for Philistine women was borne out of

God's plan to begin to deliver the children of Israel from the Philistines by the hands of their son.

Enroute with his mother and father to make the marital contract, Shimshon slew a young lion in the vineyards of Timnath, but he did not tell his parents. Upon his return to consummate the marriage, he remembered the incident and made a diversion into the vineyard to take a look at the lion's remains. He found that a swarm of bees had nested in the carcass of the lion and that there was honey in the honeycombs. Reaching in, he removed and ate some of the honey and gave some to his parents; but he refrained from telling them its source. Doing so would have raised great alarm in them. These were God-fearing parents who did everything in accordance with the conditions to be observed by a Nazarite in raising up their child. However, they did not discern that God placed only one condition upon him: "...and no razor shall come on his head: for the child shall be a Nazarite unto God from the womb" (Judges 13:5).

Seeing that he had come to claim his bride without a wedding party, the in-laws gathered thirty young men to the wedding feast to fill in as his companions. On the first day of the feast, Shimshon proposed a riddle as a challenge to his companions: if they could solve it in seven days, he would give each one a change of garments, but if not, then each one would give him a change of garments. They immediately engaged his wife to obtain the answer to the riddle. After three days with no progress, they threatened to burn her and her family with fire if she did not discover and reveal the answer to them. More desperate than ever, she pressed him continually, 'till on the seventh day he revealed his secret to her. She, in turn, revealed it to his companions, who then related the answer back to him before the day ended.

The door of opportunity being open for the Lord

to exact judgment for their transgression, the Spirit of the Lord came upon Shimshon, leading him down to Ashkelon, a city of the Philistines, where he slew thirty Philistines and divided their garments among his companions according to his word. Being still enraged at his wife's duplicity, he returned to his father's house without her. Early on, we observe the total orchestration of events in Shimshon's life by the Holy Spirit: first, he was moved to take a wife from among the Canaanites, which thing was forbidden of God; next, and just as significant, the Lord prevented him (a righteous judge) from fully taking possession of his wife and thus becoming the source of offense that would cause his people to rebel against their God.

Sometime later, during wheat harvest (May/June), Shimshon decided to make up with his wife. Amicably taking a young goat along as a gift, he arrived only to find that his father-in law had given his wife to the companion who had played the role of friend (today's best man). In the face of such an affront, Shimshon took revenge upon the Philistine people by setting their grain fields, including wheat, corn, and olive groves afire. In turn, the Philistines burned Shimshon's wife and father-in law with fire because they were the cause of his action. Now a widower, Shimshon felt justified in avenging the murder of his wife. Therefore, he strove against them to the extent that he slew a great number of them. Feeling avenged, he retreated to the top of the rock Etam, a stronghold in Judah, thinking that the matter between himself and the Philistines was settled. But having discovered his whereabouts, they arrayed themselves for battle against the tribe of Judah in Lehi. Perturbed at the might and objective of the Philistines, three thousand men of Judah went up against Shimshon with the intent of delivering him captive to their rulers. But Shimshon would not allow them to take him until they had sworn not to do him any harm themselves. Thereupon, they bound him with two new cords and delivered him to the Philistines.

Seeing their enemy and tormentor delivered to them helplessly bound, the Philistines shouted triumphantly with joy. But the Lord, taking occasion against them, came mightily upon Shimshon. Loosening the cords that bound him as though they had been scorched by fire, Shimshon seized upon the jawbone of an ass that lay nearby, and with it, slew one thousand armed Philistines. The remainder of the army fled in total disarray before him.

Coming to grips with the event that had just occurred, Shimshon could scarcely restrain himself from expressing amazement at the "heaps upon heaps" of lifeless bodies around him. Moreover, to think that so great a feat had been accomplished at his hand was unbelievable.

Soon, however, the effects of dehydration overtook Shimshon so that he was extremely faint from thirst and felt that he would die if he did not drink immediately. Therefore, he called upon the Lord who heard him and provided nourishing water, which sprang forth from a hollow in the jawbone. When he had drunk his fill, his spirit was refreshed so that he revived. Therefore, he named that place Enhakkore, which means "Fount of the Caller."

In the aftermath of all these things, Shimshon went down to Gaza, a coastal city of the Philistines. Coming across a harlot of the city, he went in and cohabited with her that night. In the meantime, the Philistines plotted how they might kill him in the morning. They surrounded his lodging place and kept the gate to the city secure in order to prevent his escape. But Shimshon arose to leave at midnight, only to discover men lying in wait to take his life. Having openly entered the stronghold of their walled city with utter disdain, what more insult could he inflict than to render them vulnerable by uprooting the two posts to the gate, including the doors and bar to the city. Not only did he uproot the entire gate system, but he put it on his shoulder and carried it miles away atop a hill before Hebron, a city that Judah had taken from the Canaanites. This was an incredible feat of strength, considering that the gates to the city were presumably reinforced with iron. The entire structure could have weighed more than a ton.

Now Shimshon did not shy away from contact with the Philistines; instead, he continued to frequent their cities. It came to pass that he met and fell in love with another Philistine woman who lived in the valley of Sorek. Her name was Delilah. At an opportune time, the lords of the Philistines united and bribed her to discover the secret to Shimshon's great strength, whereby he could be vanquished. In exchange, they would each recompense her eleven hundred pieces of silver, thus making her a wealthy woman. She undertook this task in all earnesty and succeeded in extracting the truth of the source of his great strength and how it could be neutralized.

This was the second relationship with Philistine women in which Shimshon had been deceived. The first involved his wife. He loved both women, and each one used the same weapon, nagging, to achieve her objective. In the first instance, the Timnitish wife "wept before him daily until the seventh day when he revealed the secret of his riddle, because she lay sore upon him." In the second relationship, Delilah "pressed him daily and urged him with her words until his soul was vexed unto death."

Does Scripture say in vain that it is better for a man to dwell in a corner of the rooftop than in a large house with a contentious woman (Proverbs 21:9); or, in the wilderness than with a contentious woman (Proverbs 21:19)? How about the earth being disquieted because of an odious woman when she is married (Proverbs 30:21, 23)?

After being evasive on three prior occasions, Shimshon finally took Delilah into his confidence and revealed the secret to the source of his strength. Certain this time of the information she had, Delilah sent for the lords of the Philistines and received payment for her accomplishment. Then she caused him to sleep upon her knees while she had a man shave off all seven locks of his hair. He awoke from sleep as she was afflicting him and saying, "The Philistines are upon you, Samson!" Shimshon awoke under the impression that he was actually being accosted by the Philistines and that, as usual, he would shake them off. Unfortunately, he was unaware that his hair had been shaved and the Lord, his strength, had departed from him.

Vulnerable and defenseless before them, the Philistines wasted no time in binding him with fetters of brass. They removed his eyes and then transferred him to prison in Gaza, where he was subjected to forced labor. In the meantime, his hair began to grow again, but the Philistines were not keen to prevent it.

Now, the rulers of the Philistines set in order a great sacrifice unto their god, Dagon, to rejoice in their triumph over Shimshon, the enemy of their country. As the feast progressed and their hearts grew merry, they had Shimshon brought out of prison for entertainment. The building was full of men and women and all the lords of the Philistines. In addition, there were about three thousand spectators upon the roof as Shimshon entertained. Soon Shimshon requested the lad who attended him to help him feel the pillars so that he could lean upon them, presumably, to rest. Then Shimshon called upon the Lord Jehovah to strengthen him once more so that he would be avenged for his two eyes which the Philistines had plucked out. Taking hold of the pillars, Shimshon declared, "Let me die with the Philistines." Then he exerted all the force he could muster against the pillars, and the building collapsed, killing all the lords of the Philistines and the people therein.

So the Lord honored Shimshon's prayer, and he was avenged of his enemies. In dying, he slew more Philistines than he had slain in his life. Remarkably, his brethren were able to find and recover his body for burial in the burial place of his father.[9]

Sifting the Evidence with Insight

In this and the chapters following, we will sift through the evidence pertaining to Shimshon. We make the presumption that Shimshon's parents greatly desired to have children of their own bodies. In harmony with their great desire, they petitioned the Lord, even as other childless couples of faith before them had done: Avraham (Abraham) and Sarah[10], Yitzchak (Isaac) and Rivkah (Rebekah)[11], and Ya'akov (Jacob) and Rachel.[12] Therefore, there were ample precedents of the Lord intervening in the lives of barren couples to cause them to bear children miraculously.

This appointed conception and birth was unprecedented and unusual in that never before nor thereafter has the Lord specified conditions for the mother to observe during her pregnancy. In the case of Shmu'el (Samuel), the prophet, we observe his mother vowing the vow of a Nazarite upon her firstborn son if the Lord would end her barrenness.[13] With respect to Yochanah (John), the baptizer, the conditions of his service to the Lord were defined by God: "he shall be filled with the Holy Ghost from his mother's womb; neither shall he drink wine or strong drink."[14] Similarly for Shimshon: "he shall be a Nazarite unto God from the womb and no razor shall come upon his head."[15] But remarkable in its exclusivity are the Nazarite conditions placed upon Shimshon's mother, who was not desirous of being a Nazarite. For the angel of the Lord had said unto the woman, "Behold now, thou art barren, and bearest not: but thou shalt conceive and bear a son. Now therefore beware, I pray thee, and drink not wine nor strong drink, and eat not any unclean thing."

The sudden, unexpected appearance of an angelic being who immediately begins to describe one's medical condition is enough to astonish and inspire awe. The lady's attention would have been arrested by the opening address, "Behold, now." In other words, "Consider or take stock of yourself: You are barren!" The Hebrew word, aqar, means "barren or sterile" in the generative sense. So the lady understood the angel to say, "The reason you have been unable to conceive and bear children (if she did not know it already) is because you are sterile. But now, in harmony with your godly desire, the Lord God almighty has turned your circumstance from barrenness to fruitfulness, if you would only obey. You shall conceive and bear a son, only if you absolutely refrain from drinking wine and strong drinks and eating unclean things."

Notwithstanding the prophetic emphasis "you shall," the message bespoke a fait accompli. Divine foreknowledge was saying, "Lady, you need to know this at the beginning, but I already know the ending: You shall conceive and you shall obey the Divine will in order that you will bring forth his prepared vessel." And in the course of time, the child, Shimshon, of whom the angel prophesied, "He shall be a Nazarite unto God from the womb to the day he dies," was born. [16]

The Nazarite

And the Lord spake unto Moses, saying, Speak unto the children of Israel, and say unto them, when either man or woman shall separate themselves to vow a vow of a Nazarite, to separate themselves unto the Lord: He shall separate himself from wine and strong drink, and shall drink no vinegar of wine or vinegar of strong drink, neither shall he drink any liquor of grapes, nor eat moist grapes or dried. All the days of his separation shall he eat nothing that is made of the vine tree, from the kernels, even to the husk. All the days of the vow of his separation there shall no razor come upon his head: until the days be fulfilled in the which he separated himself unto the Lord, he shall be holy and shall let the locks of the hair of his head grow. All the days that he separateth himself unto the Lord he shall come at no dead body. He shall not make himself unclean for his father or his mother, for his brother, or for his sister when they die: because the consecration of his God is upon his head. All the days of his separation he is holy unto the Lord. And if any man die very suddenly by him, and he hath defiled the head of his consecration: then he shall shave his head in the day of his cleansing, on the seventh day shall he shave it … And he shall consecrate unto the Lord the days of his separation, and shall bring a lamb of the first year for a trespass offering: but the days that were before shall be lost, because his separation was defiled.

Numbers 6:1–12

The Nazarite was an Israelite who made a vow of separation unto holiness in service unto the Lord in the presence of the priest. The priest would then make an estimation of the fees to be paid.[17] His separation included abstinence from consumption of all alcoholic beverages and anything that came from the grapevine. He would declare the length or duration of his separation and the purpose or service for which he was obligating himself from the start. During the entire time of separation, the hair of his head was allowed to grow. No hair of his head could be cut. In the event that his consecration was defiled by the cutting of the hair of his head, drinking of alcohol, touching the dead, etc., he was required to make a trespass offering to the Lord, and start all over again as a Nazarite unto the fulfillment of his vow.

It is very important to know that no vows made to the Lord should be taken lightly, and that it is of utmost importance for the Nazarite to fulfill all the days of his separation to the Lord. If he violates his separation one hundred times, then for the one hundredth and first time, he must again separate himself unto the Lord. He must fulfill the words of his vow, starting again at the beginning as though he had just begun. For the Lord, Jehovah, will not hold him guiltless, but he will require it of him.

Scripture is replete with admonitions against breaking ones vow to the Lord: "If a man vow a vow unto the Lord, or swear an oath to bind his soul with a bond; he shall not break his word, he shall do according to all that proceedeth out of his mouth" (Numbers 30:2). "When thou shalt vow a vow unto the Lord thy God, thou shalt not slack to pay it: for the Lord thy God will surely require it of thee; and it would be sin in thee. But if thou shalt forbear to vow, it shall be no sin in thee" (Deuteronomy 23:21–22).

Now, if the Lord will require a man to strictly uphold

his vow, how much more does he bind himself to fulfill the words that proceed out of his mouth? Listen to what he says, "So shall my word be that goeth forth out of my mouth: it shall not return unto me void, but it shall accomplish that which I please, and it shall prosper in the thing whereto I sent it" (Isaiah 55:11). For he who has magnified his word above his name[18] is not a man who is capable of lying; neither is he the son of man who can repent.[19] And because he can swear by none greater, God swears by himself.[20]

Appointed to
Be a Nazarite

It happened that after the children of Israel entered into the Promised Land to possess it, that the Lord, God, delivered the inhabitants of the land into their hand. But after Joshua and all that generation who knew the Lord had died, there rose up a new generation of the children of Israel who did not know the Lord firsthand. Having received their possessions, they began to dwell in the land as a loose federation of tribes, where everyone did whatever seemed right in his own sight. They transgressed the covenant God had made with their forefathers. Therefore, God's judgment allowed their enemies to vanquish and rule over them. But because of his mercy, each time they cried out to him, he, being an attentive covenant keeping God, raised up a deliverer to deliver them out of the hand of their enemies. Yet, each time the deliverer died, they returned to doing whatever got them in their predicament in the first place.[21]

This cycle had already been repeated thirteen times over approximately three hundred and fifty-odd years.

It appeared that the children of Israel could not move beyond the infancy stage in their covenant relations with God. If they ever were to fulfill the purpose for which God had entered covenant with Abram, then it was incumbent upon the Lord to take them to the next phase in his divine plan of salvation for man.

When none could be found to stand in the gap for the salvation of man, God, in the fullness of time, provided himself a lamb fit for the redemption of all mankind. So too, when one deliverer after another could not suffice to provide the breakthrough needed by Israel to move forward in God's plan of salvation, God fashioned Shimshon, an expeditionary force of one, to take them to the next level: a solitary army, united with God with singleness of goal and purpose.

When Israel sinned again, God's judgment determined that their Philistine enemy would rule over them for forty years. At the same time, however, God initiated his plan to deliver Israel from under the oppression of their enemy, the Philistines. This was a formidable foe, skilled in the fabrication of works of iron and fully armed with chariots of iron. This presented a perfect situation in which God could, in their absolute weakness and disorganization, show himself mighty in Israel's behalf; thus, being glorified in their sight and in the eyes of their enemies.

As he had inspired the patriarch, Israel (Jacob), to prophesy beforehand, so now God called forth his servant, "For lo, thou shalt conceive, and bear a son; and no razor shall come on his head: for the child shall be a Nazarite unto God from the womb" (Judges 13:5). This one had been described by the patriarch, saying, "Dan shall judge his people, as one of the tribes of Israel. Dan shall be a serpent by the way, an adder in the path, that biteth the horse heels, so that his rider shall fall backward. I have waited for thy salvation, O Lord" (Genesis 49:16–

18). It is very likely that, at the time this prophecy came forth, Israel, speaking under the inspiration of the Holy Spirit, was not fully aware of the implications of the words he spoke. If he did see into the distant future, he doubtless would have seen Shimshon, a Danite who fit this prophecy exactly.

Oftentimes, it is just as important to pay as much attention to what is written or said as it is to what is not. Reiterating what had been spoken to the woman, the angel said to Manoah, "Of all that I said unto the woman let her beware. She may not eat of any thing that cometh of the vine, neither let her drink wine or strong drink, nor eat any unclean thing: all that I commanded her, let her observe" (Judges 13:13–14). So we have no problem with respect to the woman's obligations if she would indeed give birth to a child.

The confusion centers on exactly what the call upon Shimshon's life was. This is given precisely in Judges 13:5, "For, lo, thou shalt conceive, and bear a son; and no razor shall come on his head: for the child shall be a Nazarite unto God from the womb: and he shall begin to deliver Israel out of the hand of the Philistines" (Judges 13:5). So, there you have it. Shimshon was not merely called to be a Nazarite, but he was unquestionably appointed by God, unto God, and answerable only to God. The only obligation imposed on this Nazarite was that no razor could come on his head. Notice here, that it is not said or written, "He may not eat anything that cometh from the vine, neither let him drink wine or strong drink, nor eat any unclean thing."

A few paragraphs earlier, we read God's own words describing the obligations that a man or woman took on when he or she vowed the vow of a Nazarite. They can be found in Numbers 6, and include separation from drinking alcoholic beverages, eating nothing from the vine, and touching no unclean things. Notice that these prohibitions apply to anyone who voluntarily vows the vow of a Nazarite, and not to one who is appointed by God. In appointing Shimshon to this office, God only prohibited him from ever using a razor upon his head. Understandably, as you will see, in order for this commission to take effect upon a child from the moment of conception would require proxies to fill certain roles such as the one making the vow and the priest. Both parents and God played bit roles for Shimshon while God filled in both as priest and God.

More than six hundred years before, the patriarch, Israel, spoke the fatherly blessings upon his sons. Of particular interest is the blessing he bestowed upon his son Dan because it has direct bearing on our subject, "Dan shall judge his people, as one of the tribes of Israel." We know that Israel spoke prophetically because he said to his sons, "...Gather yourselves together, that I may tell you that which shall befall you in the last days..." (Genesis 49:1). In the last days, relative to then, would be the future. And in all the years that transpired, Shimshon was the only Danite of record to judge his people. Take a few minutes to meditate upon the above passages to get them settled in your mind. Selah!

The Purpose

There was a special anointing upon Shimshon. Even before his conception, he was sanctified as a Nazarite through his mother, who was required to observe some of the same rigors of the Nazarite until he was weaned. For all the while he was nourished from her body, she was required to observe the dietary constraints of the Nazarite. His parents were charged with observing all that the angel told them concerning the child: "... And no razor shall come on his head: for the child shall be a Nazarite unto God from the womb ..." (Judges 13:5).

It was mandatory for the Nazarite to state the purpose of his separation in the presence of the priest when he appeared to make his vow. This declaration was made before commencing the days of his separation. Since Shimshon wasn't conceived yet but was supposed to begin observing the days of his separation from the womb, God spoke the purpose of his calling, saying, " ... And he shall begin to deliver Israel out of the hand of the Philistines" (Judges 13:5). Thereby, Shimshon became "the arrow of the Lord's deliverance of Israel from the Philistines."[22]

Some theologians would argue that Shimshon was denied the exercise of his free will; that he, as an unborn, was incapable of comprehending his calling or concurring with the purpose of it. Essentially, here was a baby, growing up as a child into manhood, who did not have a choice in the matter of whether or not he desired to fulfill the vow of a Nazarite his entire lifetime. Also, was God right to inject the instrument of his will into the earth realm?

We will not get caught up in the never-ending battles concerning predestination—God's foreknowledge, man's free will, etc. Rather, let us focus on Jehovah Sabbaoth, the Lord of Hosts (that is, Commander of the armies of God). Recall from your Bible studies how God found one man, Avram (Abram), who was amenable to him and entered into a covenant relationship with that man. Now, the covenant was cut between God and the spirit-controlled man (for the flesh of the man laid asleep all the while). God's dealings with man are via his spirit so that there would be perfect accountability (for man's flesh is imperfect). In the same manner, God's covenant with Shimshon was with his spirit.

Establish the Beachhead

Among the promises made to Avram, God said, "And I will make thy seed as the dust of the earth ... and in thee shall all families of the earth be blessed" (Genesis 13:16; 12:3). Being in covenant relationship with him, God was obliged to foretell the future of his descendants. "And he said unto Avram, Know of a surety that thy seed shall be a stranger in a land that is not theirs, and shall serve them; and they shall afflict them four hundred years; And also that nation, whom they shall serve, will I judge: and afterward shall they come out with great substance" (Genesis 15:13–14). So that at the appointed time, Scripture declares, "When Israel went out of Egypt, the house of Jacob from a people of strange language; Judah was his sanctuary and Israel his dominion" (Psalm 114:1–2).

Israel is a symbolic name given to Ya'akov (Jacob) and to Avraham's posterity, including Yeshua ha Mashiach. It means a ruler (prince) who has prevailed with God and man and attained power. In other words, Israels are men governed by God to rule among men on God's behalf. By extension, Israel is symbolically applicable to all who believe in the name of the Son of God, for they are empowered to become sons of God. In light of the heretical doctrine perpetrated by some that the body of Christ, the Church, is the spiritual replacement for national Israel, the Jews, care is taken here to refute such error and declare that God has called all believers to be Israels (rulers under his authority).[23] However, Gentile believers make up only a subset of the whole body of believers that include the natural descendants of Israel.

The Hebrew word, memshalah, translated here as dominion, also means "rule, to rule, government, power, or realm." In military parlance, the latter portion of Psalm 114:2 could be interpreted as, "And God's rulers among men obtained a beachhead from which his kingdom (dominion) would extend throughout the earth." The beachhead is the initial foothold or territory secured by an invading army on enemy soil from which successive incursions or advances can be made against the enemy. This is precisely what Psalm 114:1–2 is saying. Y'hudah (Judah) became his dwelling place, and Israel his government. Every legitimate government must have a realm or territory under its authority and power. Jehovah Sabbaoth accomplished this through his people, Israel, starting from the promised land. Although Israel was totally unaware of the spiritual battle going on during their early years in the promised land, God could not advance salvation to the rest of mankind beyond the physical nation until it was first established upon the beachhead that was Israel.

Hence, the Commander of the armies of God, through his covenant partners, had free reign to array his forces in battle against all opposing foes on earth, employing every strategy according to his predetermined counsel. Therefore, in the fullness of time, God, the Master Potter, fashioned a vessel of clay and appointed it to be a mighty warrior in his army. As he said, "Behold, as the clay is in the potter's hand, so are ye in mine hand, O house of Israel" (Jeremiah 18:6). And we know that the potter has power over the clay.[24] Wherefore we know that God acted righteously in the matter with Shimshon.

The Duration

The Nazarite was required to state the duration of his separation unto God when he approached to make his vow before the priest. But as we know, Shimshon was declared to be a Nazarite unto God even before he was conceived. And the declared duration of his separation spanned his entire lifetime, from the womb until his death. We also know that God foretold Shimshon's coming forth and his life's mission. Again, we know that this dedication by proxy was righteous since the Potter has power over the clay.

Now, there is the matter of a slight difference between what the angel and the woman said. In Judges 13:5, the angel of the Lord said to the woman, "For the child shall be a Nazarite unto God from the womb." In relating the visitation of the angel to her husband in the seventh verse, the woman said, "For the child shall be a Nazarite to God from the womb to the day of his death." Actually, there is no discrepancy between the two statements. The woman's statement is a true representation of the angel's. Notice in the fourteenth verse that in reiterating to Manoah what he had told the woman, the angel repeated what she could not eat or drink, and then ended by saying, "All that I commanded her let her observe." In other words, "Whatever else she told you that I said is true." By divine omniscience, the Lord, knowing what the woman had related to her husband, had no need to correct her but left standing all that she had said. And we know this to be true because Shimshon remained a Nazarite to the day of his death.

Appointed to Judge

The overriding virtue in Shimshon's appointment is his unbroken consecration as a Nazarite, regardless of the specific role or act(s) he carried out. Therefore, the guiding factor in studying the acts of Shimshon must be rooted in total acceptance of his calling as a Nazarite.

Ordinarily, in our legal system, a judge is empowered

to (1) obtain all relevant facts pertaining to a matter, and
then to discern the veracity of one part versus the other;
(2) conclude the process by weighing all evidence in the
balance in order to arrive at a righteous judgment which
is proclaimed; and, (3) execute or enforce the penalty.
The fullness of this power is reserved to God who also
delegates and empowers man via human government to
exercise this authority in his stead.[25]

Moreover, God has delegated these same attributes of
judgeship to only a few men, of which Shimshon is one.
He was called to "diyn" his people. The Hebrew word
diyn means "to rule or control, to contend for, to execute
or minister judgment, to reason or be at strife with, and
to judge as an umpire." Shimshon fully embodied these
attributes on Israel's behalf.[26]

Accentuating this call to judgeship is the name
Shimshon (derived from shemesh) which associates one
man with God. Psalm 84:11 states that "The Lord God is
a (shemesh) sun and shield: the Lord will give grace and
glory." By typology, God, the provider of life, is also the
sustainer; Shimshon, the deliverer, is also the contender
for Israel. Therefore, Shimshon is a type of Yeshua
ha Mashiach in that even as Yeshua lives evermore to
enforce his will, so the after effects of Shimshon's mission
continued on to fulfillment in Mashiach (Messiah) after
his death.

The Serpent Deliverer

The latter portion of Genesis 49:16 states, "Dan,
(referring to Shimshon) shall be a serpent by the way; an
adder in the path, that biteth the horse heels, so that his
rider shall fall backward." By direct comparison between
this passage of scripture which refers to Shimshon and

that found in Numbers 21:6–9, we find that Shimshon is a type of Mashiach by contrast. The latter Scripture recounts that the Lord sent fiery serpents among his people, which bit them and caused the death of many. Upon the intercession of Moshe (Moses), the Lord provided a way of escape. By looking upon the image of the brazen serpent set upon a standard, all who had been bitten lived. This is a portrayal of God as the serpent that saves—the one who swallows up death. In contrast, Shimshon is the adder that delivers venom to the enemy of God so that his people have respite to recover and move forward from oppression. (Observe that the rider falls backward and not forward.)

THE UNFOLDING MISSION

> For, lo, thou shalt conceive, and bear a son; and
> no razor shall come on his head: for the child
> shall be a Nazarite unto God from the womb:
> and he shall begin to deliver Israel out of the
> hand of the Philistines.

Judges 13:5

We begin our study of Shimshon's mission from the
moment of conception. The anointing of the Lord was
upon him from that moment; that is, from the instant
the fertilized egg was implanted in the womb. We can
imagine the growth and division of the zygote into
specialized body parts such as arms and legs, head with
eyes, ears, nose, and mouth, etc. And the head had no
hair thereon initially!

(This was one of the rites which the Nazarite or
one who vowed a singular vow underwent: to shave off
all hair from his head before commencing and after
completing his mission. See Acts 18:18 and 21:24). Here,
we see that Shimshon began his mission without a strand

of hair on his scalp, which corresponds directly to the rite of shaving the head. Another rite was to pay the fee according to the valuation of the individual made by the priest. Alternatively, one could bring a beast to be offered to the Lord as a burnt offering.[27] Manoah satisfied this requirement when he offered up a burnt offering before the angel of the Lord.[28] By the same token, the angel of the Lord acted as the priest who valued Shimshon and appraised the offering to be acceptable.

At the appointed time (normally forty weeks of gestation), the woman gave birth to a son and called his name Shimshon. This name is derived from the Hebrew, shemesh, which also means bright or brilliant, sun, and which may have been an allusion to the brightness of the angel as he ascended in the flame of the altar to heaven after having performed wonderously before their eyes (Manoah and wife). Remember that the father sought to honor the angel of God with food, and even inquired after his name.[29] What better way to honor someone of prominence than to memorialize him? Therefore, the name Shimshon was given in commemoration of the luminescence of the angel first, and secondly, prophetically this son was destined to be among the luminaries of Israel.

The Angel of the Lord

So, exactly who was this angel of the Lord? The woman described his countenance as "very terrible" (awe inspiring or reverential). Although she did not inquire after his name or from whence he came, it was by his countenance that she could positively identify him as a man of God who had the countenance of an angel of God. But Manoah did inquire after his name. And in response, the angel said, "Why askest thou thus after my name, seeing it is (piliy) secret" (Judges 13:18)? By this response, we can know exactly who he is.

The Hebrew word piliy is rendered "secret" here. It means wonderful, remarkable, secret, marvelous, and it could just as well have been translated wonderful in this passage. In fact, it is translated wonderful in the only other passage of Scripture where it is found. Psalm 139:6 reads, "Such knowledge is too (piliy) wonderful for me: it is high, I cannot attain unto it." So what the angel said could just as well have been translated, "Why askest thou thus after my name, seeing I am wonderful?" Everything was wonderful—his appearances, his prophecy, his countenance, even his performance.

Significance of the Name

In the Hebrew culture, the name of a person, place, or thing intrinsically contained a descriptive distinction as well as its chief character marker. From his response, the angel of the Lord was saying, "Knowing that what I have told you is wonderful and miraculous, you should not even inquire after my name." But so as not to leave any doubt, after Manoah made an offering unto the Lord, the angel performed wonderful miracles before the man and his wife. The text (Judges 13:19) says, "And the angel did wonderously..." Wonderously is from the Hebrew, pala, which means "to distinguish by accomplishing greatly difficult wonders or miracles." He intended to leave no doubt concerning his identity, preferring the performances of increasingly difficult wonders to distinguish him from any other. The first scripture that might have popped up in this couple's memory might have been, "Is anything too hard for the Lord?" (Genesis 18:14).

Remembering that the Hebrew name has a twofold

purpose—to distinguish and to characterize—we know that this angel of the Lord is the very same one who is spoken of in Isaiah 9:6, which says, "And his name shall be called Wonderful." In satisfaction of this twofold purpose, the name Shimshon highlights the likenesses Shimshon has to the Lord and predicts his future and inherent greatness.

Moving to the Beat of the Drummer

The boy, Shimshon, began to grow in stature before the Lord, and the Lord blessed him. The implications of God blessing Shimshon reveal that God was with him to teach and guide him, and he was pleased with his progress. It further reveals that he learned obedience, which was of absolute necessity for the fulfillment of his mission. Finally, we understand that Shimshon was blessed of God because he delighted himself in the Lord, "For without faith it is impossible to please God" (Hebrews 11:6).

Having proved himself to be faithful in a few things and pressing toward the mark of the high calling of God, the Spirit of the Lord began to move him. Scripture records, "And the Spirit of the Lord began to move him at times in the camp of Dan between Zorah and Eshtaol" (Judges 13:25). He began to operate in the wisdom, power, and might of the Spirit of God. In the camp of the tribe of Dan, his fame began to spread, and he began to judge his people. The Hebrew word paam, translated here as "move," means "to tap or beat regularly; to agitate; to impel; to trouble; to move or cause to move." This was a regular beating; starting off "at times" or intermittently between Zorah and Eshtaol but growing in regularity and intensity. The key here is to understand it was regular and incremental. The more Shimshon was obedient, the more obedience was required of him to the point of it becoming first nature to him. As Shimshon began to grow in his relationship with God, we see that he acted at the prompting or moving of the Holy Spirit. Therefore, it is written, "The Spirit of the Lord came mightily upon him" (Judges 14:6). Such anointing of the Spirit of God must have been so dramatic at times that some outward manifestation would have accompanied it to cause a distinction as described by Shimshon himself: "I will go out as at other times before, and shake myself" (Judges 16:9).

Let us focus on the word paam and translate it as "impel." Then we can understand it to mean that the Spirit of the Lord began to impel, compel, or drive him. This is exactly how it is with anyone whose life is consecrated to God—it is no more "my" will, but "his" will. Even as Yeshua, after he was baptized by Yochanan (John), was immediately driven into the wilderness by the Spirit of the Lord to be tempted,[30] so was Shimshon driven to perform his commands. In both cases, we witness the Spirit of God taking total control of men after their complete submission to his will.

Today, the Church is fond of saying, and I am saddened by hearing, that "the Holy Spirit is a gentleman," meaning that he will not force you to do what you don't want to do. Definitely, but only if you are not totally his! The Church today does not know what it means to be consecrated to the Lord. But check out Shimshon and Yeshua, because they knew and they were.

Consider that Jehovah Sabbaoth is the Commanding General of the armies of God. He is not a commander in chief who shies away from the frontline for his own safety. He is the five-star Lion of the tribe of Judah who "turneth not away for any." He is invincible and needs no help. He is the leader of his army; he is at the head of the charge!

According to Psalm 114:2, Judah was God's sanctuary or head of the consecration for Israel during the march into the promised land. God appointed Judah to be the lead tribe among all the tribes of Israel, signifying his presence at the head of any expedition. This would be expected, for God inhabits the praises of Israel and praises to God emanate from and abound in the sanctuary. Psalm 76:1 echoes this fact by saying, "In Judah is God known."

And he rules by commands; not by suggestions! Can you imagine the Lord commanding his troops thusly, "Follow me in this assault if you feel like it"? If earthly commanders cannot tolerate anything other than total obedience from their enlisted soldiers, why should the Church expect any less of Jehovah Sabbaoth?

As he progressed in this relationship, it is written, "The Spirit of the Lord came upon him." Then, with maturity, he exercised the specific manifestation of supernatural strength at will. He became absolutely obedient, even unto death. This exercising of superhuman strength at will was interrupted one last time when Shimshon was bound and delivered to the Philistines at Lehi. Responding to the great shout and vast numbers of Philistine warriors assembled against Shimshon, "The Spirit of the Lord came mightily upon him" once again. Probably because if at any time Shimshon needed to know that the Lord was still with him, then was the time.

In order to understand why such a dramatic anointing of the Holy Spirit upon Shimshon was necessary at that time, let us look at the following account of a similar desperate situation:

> And, behold, there came a man named Jairus, and he was a ruler of the synagogue: and he fell down at Jesus' feet, and besought him that he would come into his house: For he had one only daughter, about

twelve years of age, and she lay a dying. But as he went the people thronged him. And a woman having an issue of blood twelve years, which had spent all her living upon physicians, neither could be healed of any, came behind him, and touched the border of his garment: and immediately her issue of blood stanched. And Jesus said, Who touched me? When all denied, Peter and they that were with him said, Master, the multitude throng thee and press thee, and sayest thou, Who touched me? And Jesus said, Somebody hath touched me: for I perceive that virtue is gone out of me. And when the woman saw that she was not hid, she came trembling, and falling down before him, she declared unto him before all the people for what cause she had touched him, and how she was healed immediately. And he said unto her, Daughter, be of good comfort: thy faith hath made thee whole; go in peace. While he yet spake, there cometh one from the ruler of the synagogue's house, saying to him, Thy daughter is dead; trouble not the Master. But when Jesus heard it, he answered him, saying, Fear not: believe only, and she shall be made whole.

Luke 8:41–50

There was desperation in each situation. Jairus's only daughter had just died; on the other hand, Shimshon had just been helplessly bound and delivered to at least one thousand hostile warriors who were ready to pounce on him and tear him apart. Compounding each situation, Jairus's servant arrived and told him the disheartening news of his daughter's death while the Philistines took up a great shout of aggression against Shimshon. Being present in bodily form with Jairus, Yeshua immediately cautioned him not to abandon faith, but reassuringly said, "Fear not: believe only, and she shall be made whole" or 'Believe not, and I can do nothing." But not being physically present with Shimshon, the Lord resorted to the only way Shimshon could be absolutely certain of his presence, "The Spirit of the Lord came upon him mightily." Thereby was he reassured, "Fear not, I am always with you."

The moving of the Spirit of God upon Shimshon can be likened in purpose and effect as the moving of the pillar of cloud by day to Israel in their wilderness journey. It meant, "Attention, get up; get moving!" And move he did. He learned obedience from an early age. Each time the Spirit moved him, he did not hesitate to obey.

Returning to our chronology, Shimshon journeyed down to the Philistine city of Timnath. There, he met and fell in love with a Philistine woman. Upon his return home, he prevailed upon his parents to obtain this woman for his wife. Now, the Lord had commanded Israel not to intermarry with any of the people who dwelled in the land that he had given them, saying, "Neither shalt thou make marriages with them; thy daughter thou shalt not give unto his son, nor his daughter shalt thou take unto thy son. For they will turn away thy son from following me, that they may serve other gods: so will the anger of the Lord be kindled against you, and destroy you suddenly" (Deuteronomy 7:3–4).

Notwithstanding, the children of Israel gave their daughters in marriage to the Canaanites and received wives of the Canaanites for themselves.[31] This proved to be a snare to them in that they were repeatedly drawn away into idolatry. In response, God's anger was kindled against them. Therefore, he allowed their enemies to suppress and oppress them again and again. But being merciful and gracious, he delivered them from the oppressor whenever they repented.

After the death of Abdon, the thirteenth judge of

Israel, the children of Israel once again sinned against the Lord. This time, he did something new. Instead of waiting until Israel repented and cried out for deliverance, God began to raise up a deliverer for Israel at the same time that he allowed the Philistines to begin to exercise dominion over them.

The chronology of events was on this order: Just as the Philistines began to rule over Israel, the angel of the Lord announced the pending birth of his servant, Shimshon. He was born within the first year of the oppression. All Israeli males were eligible for military service at the age of twenty years, which was the beginning of manhood (see Exodus 30:12–14). Thus, midway through the forty years of oppression, when Shimshon had become twenty years old, the anointing of the Lord came upon him to begin delivering his people. And he contended for them for twenty years, executing judgment upon the enemies of his people. Thus, his life span totaled forty years, equal in number to the total number of years that the Philistines ruled over Israel.

Shimshon is condemned by the Christian world for having failed to accomplish his mission. Christians think that his mission was to deliver Israel from physical oppression only. No, Shimshon's mission was to begin to deliver Israel spiritually; provide temporary respite from physical oppression so that spiritual growth and national unity would begin. This seemingly unimportant qualifier cannot be de-emphasized: its placement before the word deliver has been so overlooked that its meaning has been muted all these years. The word begin is translated from the Hebrew chalal which, among other things, means to bore, to begin (to pry open as with a wedge). The idea is that once the wedge is set in place, there is no return to prior conditions—no shutting again of the door. In fact, over time, the opening gets wider until the door is fully open. What Shimshon began was continued in the prophet Shmu'el (Samuel), in King David,[32] and completed in Yeshua ha Mashiach.[33] In more precise language, Shimshon's mission was to pry open the doorway of salvation for the Lord who "openeth and no man shutteth" (Revelation 3:7).

Shimshon's first act after turning twenty was to marry a Philistine woman whom he loved. Killing the lion, an awesome feat of strength, was not insignificant either. He had always had an eye for Philistine women and never for an Israeli woman. His flabbergasted parents could only ask, "Is there never a woman among the daughters of thy brethren, or among all my people ... ?" But they were unaware that the Lord was orchestrating Shimshon's life, that he set apart this earthen vessel to do his bidding. Yet, some still contend that Shimshon disobeyed God when he took a wife from among the ungodly people who remained in the land.

First Test of Faith

When two foes have arrayed themselves in battle, the most desired outcome is for the one to prevail over the other without ever having to engage in hostilities. In other words, the objective is to cause the capitulation of the enemy before the two armies can engage. One of the most important strategic elements used to obtain this objective is psychological in nature: If you can make your opponent to mentally believe that you are his superior, you have achieved the psychological edge. For all practical purposes, the battle is yours.

Such was the case when Israel received this evil report from ten of twelve spies sent to consider possessing the land of promise, "And there we saw the giants, the sons of Anak, which come of the giants: and we were in our own sight as grasshoppers, and so were we in their sight" (Numbers 13:33). Now, how could they know this? Did they get outside of their bodies and take a look at themselves? Is it any wonder that God became so exasperated with unbelief among his people?

The devil, being crafty in his undertakings, uses psychology in either of two ways, (1) he will entice you to see the situation in a humbling way (e.g., Goliath to the armies of Israel and as illustrated by the ten spies); or (2) he will entice you to see the situation with yourself being exalted above it (e.g., the serpent and Eve in the garden of Eden). Mental acceptance of either one of his presentations means you lose and he wins because you would have rejected God's report. The first scenario leaves one reeling in self-pity; the second leaves one buried beneath his own vanities.

As stated above, this strategy is most effective when utilized before the opposing camps can engage. The devil knows this, and it is a favorite of his. If he can stare down the arrow of God and cause it to turn tail in flight, the battle is his. He tried and failed against Yosef (Joseph) and, of course, Yeshua prior to launching out in their ministries.

He tried the same strategy against Shimshon en route to Timnath to launch his ministry. There, in the vineyards of Timnath, a "young lion roared against him" (Judges 14:5-6). The Hebrew word, qirah, rendered against, means "to encounter accidentally in a friendly or hostile manner."

Please note that this lion was not described as old; he was described as a young lion! This can only mean a fully mature male lion in his prime. This was a huge and fierce beast of enormous strength, which was frightening to unexpectedly run up against. This beast did not roar "at" Shimshon; it roared against him. This roaring would have been the prelude to the charge and attack upon Shimshon. Imagine this lion openly defying God who had given man the rule over every beast in the earth! Instead of backing off in deference to the man, he chose hostility over friendliness. This animal deliberately chose not to recognize the anointing of the Holy Spirit of God upon Shimshon. Surely, this was the work of the devil.

Imagine yourself as an unarmed rookie soldier on his first military excursion who just happens to run up against the fiercest unit of the enemy. Wouldn't your first reaction be to turn tail and run or surrender immediately in an attempt to save your life? Under the pressure of the moment, Shimshon, the rookie, did not turn tail, nor panic in fear: Instead, by faith, he stood his ground against the lion, believing that what the Lord said—'you shall be a Nazarite unto me, and shall begin to deliver Israel'—he was able to perform.

Therefore, in response to the faith exhibited by Shimshon, the Spirit of the Lion of the tribe of Judah came mightily upon him, empowering him to tear the lion apart with his bare hands. Shimshon then entered into his ministry under the anointing, power, and direction of the Holy Spirit. He continued his ministry in the knowledge that he would fulfill his mission only by faith.

Vex Midian

When God sought an occasion to smite the Philistines who were among the contributing cause for him smiting Israel, he reached into his quiver and pulled out the arrow of his deliverance—Shimshon. When Yosef (Joseph) needed occasion to bind his brothers into returning with his younger brother, Binyamin (Benjamin), he returned each man's money to his sack of grain and accused them of stealing. When King Ahab sought to bend the Word of God to his own desires, God allowed a lying spirit to confirm a lie in all the prophets' mouths. In turn, they persuaded Ahab of the lie. When Midian, through Balaam's advice, vexed Israel and caused her to sin, thereby incurring the wrath of God, God later commanded Moses, "Vex the Midianites and smite them" (Numbers 25:17). So too, God found occasion to vex the Philistines and smote them with Shimshon, the arrow of his deliverance to Israel. His marriage to a Philistine woman and the slaying of the lion set the stage upon which a quarrel could be constructed in order to engage them.

Would God spend twenty years preparing an instrument of deliverance and have that instrument misfire in his hand? "Is any thing too hard for the Lord" (Genesis 18:14) or "Is the Lord's hand waxed short" (Numbers 11:23)? Consider the potter and the clay principle: the clay is put to whatever use the potter desires, and cannot say "I will not be put to such and such a use." You may see disobedience in Shimshon's actions, but he was always obedient to the moving of the Spirit. In other words, he was compelled or impelled into action. And scripture records, "But his father and his mother knew not that it was of the Lord, that he sought an occasion (an opening) against the Philistines" (Judges 14:4). This single statement is a witness that Shimshon was not a misfired arrow, but one that was aimed at and delivered into the heart of the Philistines. Through Shimshon, Jehovah Sabbaoth was orchestrating a proven strategy: vex the enemy into committing an offense in order to have justification for exercising judgment upon him.

Plowing of the Wicked

The stage was set when Shimshon's companions conspired with his wife to discover the answer to his riddle. He immediately knew the source of their discovery when they correctly told him the answer to the riddle before the seventh-day deadline expired. In response, Shimshon accused them of duplicity by conspiring with his young, immature wife. Specifically, he said "If ye had not plowed with my heifer, ye had not found out my riddle." Seizing the occasion, the Spirit of the Lord led him down to Ashkelon, a city of the Philistines, where he slew and took spoil from thirty of them. These, he divided among his companions to honor the promise he had made to them. Then being rather angry against his wife, he departed from her and returned to his father's house alone.

The word plowed is translated from the Hebrew, charash, which means "to plow, scratch, or engrave by means of a tool." It denotes fabricating or devising in a bad sense with all intent toward concealment or secrecy. This is confirmed by scripture in Proverbs 21:4 which says, "The plowing of the wicked is sin." The word heifer is well known to mean a not fully-grown or immature cow as opposed to a bull (and the inference is clear).

Shimshon was fully justified in doing what he did. First, as a Nazarite, he was righteous and holy unto God. Then, as a righteous judge before God, he was empowered to fully judge a matter, even as God by discerning the facts, rendering a verdict, and executing the sentence. In fact, he was "the minister of God, a revenger to execute wrath upon him who doeth evil" (Romans 13:4). All this was prophesied by the patriarch, Israel, when he said, "Dan shall judge his people, as one of the tribes of Israel" (Genesis 49:16). The Hebrew word, diyn, or duwn, translated "judge" in this passage is used only of God and men in authority. It means "to rule or control, to contend for, execute or minister judgment, reason, be at strife with, and to judge as an umpire." Shimshon's role as a judge over Israel was not to proclaim the Word of God as Samuel or Deborah did, but to contend against outsiders and minister judgment in behalf of his oppressed people. And for twenty years, he did such an outstanding job, so pleasing to the Lord that the honor of being mentioned among the elders of faith was conferred upon him in the book of Hebrews.

The Avenger

In offending Shimshon, the Philistines violated two commands of God: (1) "For a man shall leave father and mother and cleave to his wife, and they shall be one flesh," and (2) "Thou shalt not (lie) bear false witness." They undermined Shimshon's relationship with his young and inexperienced wife. Secondly, they were duplicitous in the matter of discovering the answer to his riddle. Notwithstanding, Shimshon was faithful to honor his word to them even as God would. On the other hand, he was obligated to execute judgment upon them because of his calling as God's proxy on the earth.

A Sun and Shield

The full significance of the naming of Shimshon (Shemesh: sun, light) and the mandate as a Nazarite of God to judge his people can be discerned by the corroboration of two passages of Scripture: In Genesis 49:16, it is written, "Dan shall judge (diyn: umpire, contend for, be at strife with, and execute judgment) his people..." while in Psalm 84:11, "...God is a sun (shemesh: sun, sustainer, provider) and shield (magen: ruler, protector, defense, shield, buckler). Recalling that in the Hebrew culture the name of a person fulfilled a dual purpose, it is plain to see the attributes of God as sun (rule and sustain) and shield (provide respite from physical oppression) manifested in Shimshon the judge (diyn: executor of judgment).

By no stealth of his, the enemy failed to discover what Shimshon had done when he slew thirty men of Ashkelon. So, another occasion was needed to continue prying apart the doorway of salvation. That opportunity presented itself soon enough when he returned to reconcile with his estranged wife.

Because his anger was kindled against her while he was away, Shimshon's father-in-law gave his bride as wife to the companion whom he had used as his friend. Therefore, the father would not permit Shimshon to reconcile with his wife; instead, he offered the younger, fairer-looking sister as a replacement bride. For many men, this would have been an agreeable exchange. But for Shimshon, a righteous judge and Nazarite before the Lord, this would have been a transgression of the Lord's command, "Neither shall thou take a wife to her sister, to vex her, to uncover her nakedness, beside the other in her lifetime" (Leviticus 18:18). No doubt, he would have been rendered impotent as a judge had he acquiesced in such a nefarious scheme.

According to the manner of man, if a judge's judgment might be compromised by special interest, he must recuse himself from a case; neither can one who is guilty of a fault sit in judgment over another. But a righteous judge—what will render him impotent in judging a matter? Therefore, Shimshon said, "Now shall I be more blameless than the Philistines, though I do them a displeasure" (Judges 15:3). Accordingly, acting instead of God, Shimshon quickly decided the matter, rendered a verdict, and proceeded to execute the judgment. Now, what judge is guilty because he decides a matter and renders a sentence according to law? And what enforcer is guilty of the law because he enforces the judge's sentence according to the law? Isn't God allowed to place all of these responsibilities under the authority of one individual?

When the Philistines learned that Shimshon had destroyed their crops in the field with fire because of the matter concerning his wife, they in turn burned both father and daughter with fire. This punishment was meant to serve as a deterrent to any Philistine who would act in such a manner, but especially as vindication to placate Shimshon for the wrong which had been done to him. Unfortunately, the Philistines failed to realize the full ramification of what they had done. They had murdered the wife of a man who had the wherewithal to exact vengeance upon them. For he said, "Though you have done this, yet will I be avenged of you, and after that I will cease" (Judges 15:7).

The Bible says that he "smote them with a great slaughter," and then, being content with the vengeance he had wreaked, Shimshon went and dwelled in the top of the rock Etam, which was a stronghold of the tribe of Judah. In hot pursuit, the Philistines set up their base in Judah and arrayed themselves in Lehi against Judah. They communicated that the reason for their battle array was to capture Shimshon in order to take revenge upon him for what he did to them. Not without his permission, the men of Judah bound him with two new cords before delivering him to their rulers, the Philistines. At the sight of their enemy bound and set before them, the Philistines shouted with a great shout of triumph. Whereupon, the Spirit of the Lord came mightily upon Shimshon and enabled him to slay a thousand warriors with nothing more than the jawbone of an ass.

What a mighty and wonderful testimony! Imagine, if you will, one man against an army of more than a thousand men equipped with spears, swords, and shields on horses and in chariots of iron. This was an army that struck fear in the hearts of three thousand of his kinsmen and caused them to betray him. Then imagine the impossible: this man, with a loud shout and mighty shaking, seizes upon the jawbone of an ass lying nearby and with it, begins to wreak havoc upon his enemies! Every soldier it seems is running to and fro, into each other, trying to escape from this lone dervish who appears to be everywhere at the same time. The more they trip and fall over each other, the easier prey they become to him. All the while, he uses only the jawbone as a weapon because his hand has cleaved to it. It is impossible to let go of it! And, impossibility of impossibilities, at the end of it all, there was not a single scratch or wound inflicted upon his body; neither was a single strand of hair cut off his head! And there, retreating in the distance before him was the once-proud Philistine army, limping hurriedly away in great disorder as though being pursued. What a great and glorious miracle! Shimshon could not help but honor the Lord. Therefore, he sanctified the place and renamed it Ramath Lehi, High Place of the Jawbone, instead of the former name Lehi, or Jawbone.

Then, being weary from such tremendous physical exertion and faint from thirst, Shimshon gave praise to God, calling upon the Lord for water. In response to his faithful servant, the Lord caused a fountain of nourishing water to spring up out of a hollow part of the jawbone that Shimshon had cast from his hand. Now revived by the refreshing spring of water, Shimshon again honored the Lord by calling the name of this other location Enhakkore, or Fount of the Caller. Contrary to the assertion by Josephus[34] that Shimshon, being filled with pride, attributed this victory to himself, we turn to none other but Scripture for verification. Judges 15:18 reads, "And he was sore athirst, and called on the Lord and said, Thou hast given this great deliverance into the hand of thy servant: and now, shall I die for thirst, and fall into the hand of the uncircumcised?" How does a servant call upon his master: in pride or humility? In all this, Shimshon manifested meekness, being mindful always of the source of his blessings.

Just prior to his death and to the children of Israel entering the promised land, Moses, the servant of God, blessed them and spoke these words concerning the tribe of Dan, "Dan is a lion's whelp: he shall leap from Bashan" (Deuteronomy 33:22). Although he never before had shown any fear of the Philistine enemy, we find Shimshon, after his victory over them at Ramath Lehi, frequenting their territory more and more. Even as it is said, "The lion is strongest among beasts, and turneth not away for any" (Proverbs 30:30), so Shimshon, the strong, lionhearted servant of God, proved true to his character. Not only did the prophecy of Israel fit him to a tee, but also that of Moses; for we see Shimshon exhibiting great strength, fearlessness, tenacity, resoluteness, and singular expansion of his territory. Collectively, the tribe of Dan did unilaterally expand its territory á la Shimshon, but at a later time.

After defeating and setting the Philistine army in disarray, Shimshon ventured down into the Philistine seacoast city of Gaza. This was a walled and gated stronghold of the Philistines. Upon entering the city, Shimshon came across a harlot and went in unto her. Presumably, his entry time would have been after dusk because the Gazites surrounded the place where he lodged, posting guards at the city gates with the intent of killing him in the morning. But under the moving of the Holy Spirit, Shimshon rose up to leave at midnight.[35] Scripture is silent concerning a struggle between himself and those who laid in wait for his life. Nonetheless, in the process of leaving, he uprooted the two posts that anchored the city gates, plus its doors and bar. He hoisted these on his shoulders and transported them many miles away into territory settled by the tribe of Judah. This is called "making a show of them openly."[36] He not only defeated them and entered boldly into their stronghold, but he also left them exposed to attack by any invader when he removed their security and first line of defense.

Later on in his life, Shimshon again boldly entered and lived in Philistine territory. This time, he fell in love with another Philistine woman who lived in the valley of Sorek. Her name was Delilah. Contrary to popular speculation, she was not a harlot. At least Scripture does not identify her as such. The worst that can be said of her is that she betrayed her lover for a goodly sum of money. Alternatively, by building upon another hint of Scripture, we can conclude that she was a weaver. In verses thirteen and fourteen of Judges 16, Shimshon mentions that if Delilah would weave the seven locks of his hair with the web of the loom, he would become vulnerable and weak. Being a weaver, she was able to perform this and then undo the weaving without having to put a razor to the hair of his head. By this, we know that this woman functioned in an honorable profession as a weaver. But that did not prevent her from betraying a loving relationship with Shimshon to the nefarious plans of the Philistine rulers for silver. The lords of the Philistines took advantage of the opportunity to discover the source of Shimshon's great strength through his relationship with Delilah. They entered into an arrangement with her that if she could entice him to reveal the secret of his strength and how they could overcome him, she would receive eleven hundred pieces of silver from each one of them (a high price, which translated to 5,500 pieces of silver).

Delilah set out to earn herself a fortune. In the ensuing days, she began to ask him to tell her the secret to his great strength and how he might be vanquished. He brought her to complete exasperation through three jesting episodes in which he supposedly revealed his secret. On the first two occasions, she had men staged and at the ready to subdue him, in the event he did reveal his secret. She would playfully flail at him while he slept, and say, "The Philistines be upon thee, Shimshon" (Judges 16:9, 20). After the third occasion, she became desperate. Using the same strategy employed by his late wife, and with the same result, she pressured him incessantly until his very soul was vexed unto death.

The Sacrifice

This vexing of his spirit unto death does not speak of an easy resignation or a ready capitulation to an awesome, overwhelming force; neither does it speak of futility in his life. Undoubtedly, Delilah's constant and persistent nagging triggered the answer in his spirit to the call from his Master that now was the appointed time to lay down his life (this, his fortieth year marked the end of Israel's oppression). Until then, he had no desire to die; everything was going well. He was in love again, and he had grown up into a mature relationship with the Spirit of the Lord. Dying was definitely not on the horizon. But all of a sudden, his very soul was desirous of death; yet, strangely, it grieved him to die.

This is what the sacrifice is all about: One offering a precious item of one's own possession to another of higher power in satisfaction of an obligation to affect a change for the better. This is what it (the vexing of his soul) speaks of—sacrifice. It is about surrendering your darling, your one and only, to the will and power of the most Benevolent One. It certainly is not an inviting thing to do to lose your life; but looking beyond that and putting his trust in the goodness and power of the Lord, Shimshon was obedient unto a vicarious death.

In the same manner, in the garden of Gethsemane, Yeshua, the Lamb that was slain from before the foundation of the world, entered into a similar situation that required him not only to offer up his darling, but to also submit to a lesser power—death. Scripture records this conflict with Yeshua saying, "My soul is exceeding sorrowful unto death..." (Matthew 26:38). His life was not taken away from him; rather, through obedience he laid down something too precious to valuate. And not for his benefit, but for the benefit of others including those who hate him. So, there he was in Gethsemane at a crossroad, wrestling with something so alien it would make your skin creep. His sweat was as great droplets of blood oozing forth from his flesh, attesting to the enormity of his struggle. "And he said, Abba, Father, all things are possible unto thee; take away this cup from me: nevertheless not what I will, but what thou wilt" (Matthew 26:39). So in obedience to the Divine will, "He humbled himself and became obedient unto death, even the death of the cross" (Philippians 2:8).

Yielding to the divine will meant that Yeshua would partake of and surrender to something so alien to his divine nature, it was abhorrent to consider. Imagine, if you can, the lion that is the strongest among beasts and fears none just giving in to another beast without a fight? Then, can you imagine the omnipotent God becoming impotent and capitulating to his enemy? Yes, surrendering meant bowing to death, the last enemy of God to be destroyed.

Implicitly, this did not only mean becoming sin and deserving of death, but also being at enmity with himself, Jehovah. The enormity of such a decision is seen in the great droplets of blood which oozed out of his pores as he sweated in Gethsemane. Mark 14:33–35 describes this enormity as him being "very heavy and sore amazed." So much so that going forward a little, he fell on the ground and prayed, "Father, all things are possible unto thee; take away this cup from me." He was literally in a terrible state of shock. Commenting on this same moment of agony, Hebrews 5:7 informs us that he offered up prayers with strong crying and tears that he should be saved from (eternal) death. And as always, without fail, the Father granted the request of the Son to save him from that which he feared (eternal alienation from the Godhead). In the balance hung the salvation of all the souls of men as opposed to that of his own. And he chose enmity with God in order to save his creation. Hallelujah! In other words, he, by opposing himself, was reconciling the lost and perverted world back to himself. He not only was the final atonement, but also the peace offering—the door of entry into the atonement.

Let us now return to the Shimshon account. Unable to constrain himself any longer, he poured out his heart to her, "There hath not come a razor upon mine head; for I have been a Nazarite unto God from my mother's womb: if I be shaven, then my strength will go from me, and I shall become weak, and be like any other man" (Judges 16:17). These words were not spoken blandly, but with conviction and finality, even as Yeshua said to Judas, "That which you must do, do thou quickly" (John 13:27). Then, she, not sparing, sent and called for the lords of the Philistines. However, she, like all of Christendom, did not realize that he was appointed a Nazarite from the womb to the day he died, just as his mother had said before.

In a Figure

Close to one thousand years before, Avraham, when test-ed, offered up his only begotten son, Yitzchak (Isaac), be-lieving that God was able to raise him up from the dead. Through faith, Avraham received his dead son alive again unto himself in a figure. Likewise, Shimshon, being fully at peace with the one who moved him to that place of absolute obedience, felt no compunction in surrendering his darling to the Almighty.

In harmony with the divine will and at the appointed time, Shimshon's soul was vexed unto death. Being agree-able and ready to lay down his life, the Holy Spirit would have to depart from him in order to facilitate this. For while his consecration remained, he, by the power of the Holy Spirit, was invincible. Notice what Shimshon said, "If I be shaven, then my strength (the Holy Spirit) will go from me, and I shall become weak and be like any other man." In other words, unlike other men, he could not be afflicted or vanquished without being shaven. The word translated as weak, chalah, means "appointed to afflic-tion." Therefore, without imputation of sin, Shimshon was not appointed to affliction, nor could he be afflicted like ordinary men with sickness, death, etc., except some-one put a razor to his head.

This being the case, the Spirit of the Lord could not depart from him while he yet remained a Nazarite in good standing, holy unto God. However, the impasse could be broken if he died "very suddenly" in a figure, thereby defil-ing the consecration on his head. Again, this was orches-trated by the Lord.

Only one other has felt the same heaviness unto death as Shimshon. In the Garden of Gethsemane, Yeshua said, "My soul is exceeding sorrowful, even unto death," even as Shimshon's soul was vexed unto death. Interestingly, the

Hebrew word, *qatsar*, which is translated here as "vexed," is exactly equivalent to the Greek word, *perilupos*, which is translated as "exceeding sorrowful." Both of these men were so consecrated to the Lord that at the appointed time neither one thought it unworthy to lay down his life according to the predetermined counsel of God. Not only was Shimshon gravely grieved, but the full import of the Hebrew is that his soul was completely docked off or blocked off (no chance of turning back) from life. In other words, he literally died in a figure at that instant. Also in a figure, the Lord imputed sin unto Shimshon in that instant, making it possible for the final act in Shimshon's life to unfold.

Within the framework of the Nazarite ordinance, the head of his consecration is defiled if any man died suddenly because of him. Consequently, he must undergo cleansing and shave off his hair on the seventh day after. This is exactly what happened to Shimshon. He died figuratively by himself, very suddenly. Regardless of the fact that Shimshon acted in obedience to God's will, he sinned in the matter of his vicarious death. This is the only time sin was imputed to Shimshon. His soul longed and pined in submission unto death, the enemy of God. Thereby, he became sin because God is life and death is alien to him. In fact, Yeshua states in Matthew 22:32 that "God is not the God of the dead, but of the living." Clearly, his associations are only with the living and not with the dead. Therefore, spiritually, the Holy Spirit departed for an instant from Shimshon so that Delilah could set in motion just what she needed to do. Then began the cleansing process, spiritually, culminating in the shaving of his head on the seventh day. But early the morning of the eighth day, unbeknownst to anyone including Shimshon, the Holy Spirit returned and sanctified his head anew. The former days of his separation were now completely lost to him! As far as the east is from the west,[37] so were they cast into the depths of the sea.[38] The eighth day began renewal of his separation as a Nazarite unto God.

Realizing that his life was now in her hand, Delilah did not spare. Instead, she immediately sent for the lords of the Philistines to come that she should deliver their tormentor onto them. After she received payment at their hand, Delilah lulled Shimshon to sleep, and then had a man shave off all seven locks of his hair (no doubt, on the seventh day after revealing his secret). She then began to beat on him while saying "The Philistines be upon thee, Shimshon." Waking up from sleep and not realizing that he had been shaven, Shimshon said, "I will go out as at other times before, and shake myself" (Judges 16:20). But he knew not that the Spirit of the Lord, his strength, had departed from him.

This shaking spoken of here by Shimshon actually described the mighty coming of the Spirit of the Lord upon him. It is translated from the Hebrew, *na'ar*, which is used to describe the accompanying rustling of the lion's mane when he roars and shakes himself. This is reminiscent of your modern-day comic book superhero just before he is transformed into an invincible superhuman. Imagine the fear and apprehension that gripped the enemy when they heard and saw Shimshon violently shake himself while roaring at the top of his lungs before annihilating them!

But not this time. This time, the Philistines prevailed over the hapless Shimshon. They removed his eyes, bound him with fetters of brass, and imprisoned him in Gaza (this same Gaza was the site of one of his most memorable exploits, in which he made an open show of his enemies) to hard labor. Now, he became their open show as he was made to toil and perform for them. Soon, his hair began to grow during his imprisonment, but they were not aware of its significance.

Now, the Lord had made provision for sanctifying the Nazarite whose consecration had been defiled;[39] even as he made provision for the believer who sinned to be forgiven and cleansed from all unrighteousness.[40] Essentially, the Nazarite would undergo a seven-day period of ceremonial cleansing. On the seventh day, his head was shorn of all hair. On the eighth day, atonement was made for him by the priest (the Holy Spirit in this case), who also sanctified his head. All past sins were now forgiven him; however, the previous days of his separation were null and void. He therefore had to renew his vow and begin his separation all over again. So, Shimshon being shorn by Delilah, presumably on the seventh day after he revealed the secret to his great strength, would have been spiritually sanctified by God the following (eighth) day.

Sanctification

Respectively, the Hebrew and Greek words qadosh and hagiazo mean "to separate or set apart from a profane to a sacred purpose." Sanctification comes about in continued obedience to the command of God or by the choice and desire of man. The process always involves some preparation leading to sanctification, such as physical cleansing accompanied by profession of words with corresponding action. The ultimate goal of sanctification is holiness unto God through obedience. As it is written, "And ye shall keep my statutes, and do them: I am the Lord which sanctify you" (Leviticus 20:7–8). This is a twofold process: (1) man's obedience or desire in line with God's will, and (2) God's seal of grace. By this, man is enabled to continue in sanctification. By the will of God,

Shimshon was sanctified and anointed from his mother's womb, even as Jeremiah was.[41]

The Grand Finale

Then one day, all the lords of the Philistines gathered themselves together to celebrate and offer sacrifices unto Dagon, their god. Because they said, "Our god hath delivered into our hands our enemy, and the destroyer of our country, which slew many of us" (Judges 16:24). And when their hearts were merry, they summoned Shimshon out of the prison and into their midst, to provide their entertainment. The temple in which they celebrated was full of men and women, including all the lords of the Philistines. The roof held an additional three thousand men and women spectators. Inexplicably, they stationed him between the two columns that supported the building. Seizing the opportunity, Shimshon instructed the young man who led him to position his two hands upon the two columns and allow him to rest. Thereupon, he called on the Lord, saying, "O Lord God, remember me, I pray thee, and strengthen me, I pray thee, only this once, O God, that I may be at once avenged of the Philistines for my two eyes. Let me die with the Philistines" (Judges 16:28, 30). Exerting pressure against the two inner columns, he braced himself and pushed with all his might, dislodging them and causing the temple to collapse upon itself. All within were killed.

Notice that in his grand finale, Shimshon exemplified meekness and was not presumptuous. Instead of taking matters into his own hand, he dutifully and obediently petitioned the Lord to use his power. The use of God's power here, emphatically confirms that Shimshon not only remained a Nazarite unto God 'till death, but he also possessed the full attributes of his judgeship all along. In Deuteronomy 32:35, God proclaims "To me belongeth vengeance, and recompense..." Referring to this passage in Romans 12:19, Shaul (Paul) warns us, ordinary people of God, saying, "Dearly beloved, avenge not yourselves, but rather give place to wrath: for it is written, Vengeance is mine; I will repay, saith the Lord." In granting Shimshon's request to be avenged of the Philistines, God testified that Shimshon still operated under the full power and authority of a judge and Nazarite.

Although he died very suddenly in a figure, death did not manifest immediately in the natural. Until he actually yielded up his spirit, even as Yeshua did when hanging on the cross (he said, "Father, into thy hands I commend my spirit," see Luke 23:46), he could not die. Therefore, he obediently acquiesced unto death, saying, "Let me die with the Philistines" (Judges 16:30).

So the Lord granted the desire of his faithful servant, whose soul was vexed unto death. In dying, he slew upward of three thousand people, including all the lords of the Philistines. As it is written, "Dan (Shimshon) is an adder in the path, that biteth the horse heels, so that his rider shall fall backward" (Genesis 49:17). In dying, he cut off the "head" of the Philistine people, leaving them without leadership, so that Israel might have respite, in which to organize herself into the viable beachhead from whence God's sanctuary and dominion would be established and spread throughout the earth.

The Author
and Finisher

And the Lord spake unto Moses, saying, Speak unto the children of Israel, and say unto them, when either man or woman shall separate themselves to vow a vow of a Nazarite, to separate themselves unto the Lord: He shall separate himself from wine and strong drink, and shall drink no vinegar of wine or vinegar of strong drink, neither shall he drink any liquor of grapes, nor eat moist grapes or dried. All the days of his separation shall he eat nothing that is made of the vine tree, from the kernels, even to the husk. All the days of the vow of his separation there shall no razor come upon his head: until the days be fulfilled in the which he separated himself unto the Lord, he shall be holy and shall let the locks of the hair of his head grow. All the days that he separateth himself unto the Lord he shall come at no dead body. He shall not make himself unclean for his father or his mother, for his brother, or for his sister when they die: because the consecration of his God is upon his head. All the days of his separation he is holy unto the Lord. And if any man die very suddenly by him, and he hath defiled the head of his consecration: then he shall shave his head in the day of his cleansing, on the seventh day shall he shave it. And on the eighth day he shall bring two turtles, or two young pigeons, to the priest, to the door of the tabernacle of the congregation: And the priest shall offer the one for a sin offering, and the other for a burnt offering, and make an atonement for him, for that he sinned by the dead, and shall hallow his head that same day. And he shall consecrate unto the Lord the days of his separation, and shall bring a lamb of the first year for a trespass offering: but the days that were before shall be lost, because his separation was defiled.

Numbers 6:1–12

Shimshon's strength, the Spirit of the Lord, departed from him in a tangible way as soon as a razor was applied to shave the hair off his head because his consecration was defiled. God is not a respecter of persons; therefore, the Holy Spirit will not abide un-holiness, not even in God himself. Yeshua ha Mashiach was smitten with sin and became sin for us in an instant of time in order for him to bear our sins away. And during that moment, he cried out, "My God, my God, why hast thou forsaken me?" (Matthew 27:46). Therefore, the Holy Spirit would just as well have departed from Shimshon had he defiled his consecration in any way that was forbidden prior to this incident. If he had been forbidden to touch any dead thing, to eat or drink anything from the vine, and had done anything forbidden, the Holy Spirit would have departed from him without exception. By this one characteristic of God, we can know that the standard Nazarite conditions were not incumbent on him. However, he operated within the general framework of the ordinance governing the Nazarite. The singular condition placed upon Shimshon from among the standard conditions imposed by God upon anyone who voluntarily vowed to be a Nazarite, was, "...no razor shall come on his head: for the child shall be a Nazarite unto God from the womb" (Judges 13:5).

It is of primary importance to commit to memory the fact that Shimshon did not make a vow either voluntarily or involuntarily, neither did his parents promise him to the Lord, as in the case of Shmu'el's mother. Of no relevance were the drinking of wine or strong drink, or the eating of anything from the vine, or the touching of dead things. In fact, the eating of the unclean thing is not even mentioned among the conditions that the Nazarite must observe. That condition was placed upon Shimshon's mother. Nevertheless, it is commanded of God's people, whether Nazarite or not. The only condition placed upon Shimshon was that no razor should come upon his head. The Nazaritic conditions mandate that if the consecration was defiled then the Nazarite would have to cleanse himself, shave off all of his hair, and offer up a trespass offering. We know that Shimshon did none of these, and not because he was unable to, but because they were not applicable.

The Guarantor

God was the party responsible to ensure that Shimshon remained a Nazarite. He made that guarantee by saying, "For the child shall be a Nazarite to God from the womb to the day of his death" (Judges 13:7). Notice that God spoke emphatically, "the child shall be," and not "might be." Scripture records in Luke 8:22–25 another guarantee that God spoke:

Now it came to pass on a certain day, that he went into a ship with his disciples: and he said unto them, Let us go over unto the other side of the lake. And they launched forth. But as they sailed he fell asleep: and there came down a storm of wind on the lake; and they were filled with water, and were in jeopardy. And they came to him, and awoke him, saying, master, master, we perish. Then he arose, and rebuked the wind and the raging of the water: and they ceased, and there was a calm. And he said unto them, Where is your faith?

Luke 8:22–25

Almighty God spoke to his understudies, saying, "Come with me to the other side of the lake," but when they felt that their lives were in jeopardy, they feared that they would never reach the other side as the Lord had told them. Fear is unbelief. This prompted Yeshua to ask them, "Where is your faith?" There should have been no doubt about their safe journey over to the other side. The Creator of the universe spoke the end thing from before they set sail. Whatsoever thing he speaks will definitely happen and cannot be changed by anyone else. That's why his name is Amen, or So Be It! So whatever he foretold concerning Shimshon was guaranteed!

Interestingly enough, God boldly spoke two guarantees with respect to Shimshon: first, that Shimshon would be a Nazarite from the womb to death; secondly, that he would begin to deliver Israel out of the hand of the Philistines. Therefore, the Lord did not make his calling and mission conditional upon anything! Actually, God made himself the guarantor of the calling and completion of Shimshon's mission, even as he is the author and finisher of our faith, when he said, "For the child shall be a Nazarite unto God from the womb, and he shall begin to deliver Israel from out of the hand of the Philistines."

Concerning the Nazarite, the Lord said, "All the days of his separation he is holy unto the Lord" (Numbers 6:8). According to the angel of the Lord, that separation began at conception and ended at death for Shimshon. In other words, a Nazarite could not continue in his separation without abiding in holiness. Therefore, Shimshon could not remain a Nazarite from the womb to death when he supposedly committed sins which were imputed to him. Scripture informs us that there is such a man that the Lord would keep blameless, "Blessed is the man unto whom the Lord imputeth not iniquity, and in whose spirit there is no guile" (Psalm 32:2). I submit that Shimshon's spirit was truly and fully submitted to the Lord, and in him there was no guile.

When his heart desired to marry a Philistine woman, he insisted on everything being aboveboard and open to the scrutiny of all Israel; again, he was aboveboard to openly declare his judgments before executing them in the matter when his wife was given to another, and when she was burned to death by the Philistines. Neither was he slack or slothful, but he attended diligently to perform whatever he spoke. He maintained keen integrity between what he said and what he did, precisely because of the absence of guile in his heart. This caused him to be vulnerable and easy prey to the deceitful wiles of his Philistine women. He possessed the full embodiment of *agape* toward each of them and rightly expected to receive the full measure of love returned from each. Having a spirit that was so foreign to guile, Shimshon was a sitting duck, so to speak. Now, this was not an oversight by the all-wise God! Instead, it was part of his overall orchestration of the spread of his kingdom in the earth.

If one is the author as well as the finisher of a work, does that not settle the fact that that same one is also sustainer of the work? So, since the Lord is guarantor that

Shimshon remained a Nazarite throughout his life, he is guarantor also of his holiness, since without unbroken holiness one cannot continue as a Nazarite.

Remember that the Spirit of the Lord was in constant contact with Shimshon except during the seven-day period after revealing his secret to Delilah. Judges 13:25 says that the Spirit of the Lord began to move him at times. This implies that the moving was ongoing. We also remember that move means a regular beating or tapping. Altogether, we can picture Shimshon tethered to the Holy Spirit, who pulled the string at his good pleasure. He was a gift of deliverance given upon the altar to Israel. Consider what God said to Moses concerning the altar, "Seven days thou shalt make an atonement for the altar, and sanctify it; and it shall be an altar most holy: whatsoever toucheth the altar shall be most holy" (Exodus 29:37). Now, consider Shimshon, God's gift of deliverance to Israel, upon that altar. Do you get the picture? Shimshon was constantly in contact with the altar. Consequently, he was holy always before the Lord except during the interim when the consecration of the Lord upon his head was defiled according to God's plan. Nevertheless, on the eighth day thereafter, the Holy Spirit sanctified Shimshon and consecrated his head anew. Thus, God fulfilled his obligation to Shimshon, which his mother was a witness to, that the child shall be a Nazarite to God from the womb to the day of his death.

And treating on how Shimshon's sanctification was restored, the Lord repeatedly says throughout Scripture that, "I am the Lord that sanctify." Even as the word of the Lord that came to Jeremiah, "Before I formed thee in the belly I knew thee: and before thou camest forth out of the womb I sanctified thee, and I ordained thee"[42] to be a "Nazarite unto God from the womb, and to begin to deliver Israel from out of the hands of the Philistines"[43] was no less meant for Shimshon as well. For so saith the Lord, "I will have mercy on whom I will have mercy, and I will have compassion on whom I will have compassion" (Exodus 33:19; Romans 9:15). Again, he saith, "Who will lay anything to the charge of God's elect? It is God that justifieth" (Romans 8:33).

Now if there is any lingering doubt that Shimshon was holy before the Lord, consider the words of Yeshua, "Ye fools and blind: for whether is greater, the gift, or the altar that sanctifieth the gift?" (Matthew 23:19). Are there any sins committed by Shimshon, the Lord's servant, so vile that the sovereign Lord cannot cleanse? But take heed and "Accuse not a servant unto his master, lest he curse thee, and thou be found guilty" (Proverbs 30:10). For "Who art thou that judgest another man's servant?" (Romans 14:4).

MISSION
ACCOMPLISHED

Checkmate

Now, let us make a direct scriptural comparison between Shimshon's commissioning and God's ordinance for anyone who would make the voluntary vow to be a Nazarite. With respect to the yoke placed upon Shimshon, the angel of the Lord said:

> Behold now, thou art barren, and bearest not: but thou shalt conceive, and bear a son. Now therefore beware, I pray thee, and drink not wine nor strong drink, and eat not any unclean thing: For, lo, thou shalt conceive, and bear a son; and no razor shall come on his head: for the child shall be a Nazarite unto God from the womb: and he shall begin to deliver Israel out of the hand of the Philistines.
>
> Judges 13:3–5

We note that in the above dialogue, the word of the Lord was directed at two persons. First, the mother to be was forewarned not to drink wine or alcoholic beverage, nor to eat any unclean thing from that time forward until her child was weaned. The second portion of the directive was to both mother and son. The son, yet to be born, had been appointed by God to function in the office of a Nazarite unto God throughout his lifetime. The mother was to ensure that no razor was used on his head while he was a child, with that responsibility reverting to him when he became of age. Finally, his mission as a Nazarite was defined: To begin to deliver his people from out of the hand of their Philistine oppressors.

Turning our attention to the full ordinance specifying what conditions must be met and maintained by one desirous of becoming a Nazarite, we notice there are three main ones. First, he must forego ingesting, either by drinking or eating, anything from the grape vine. Secondly, he must not allow any razor to be applied to his head. Finally, he must neither mourn nor come nigh the dead; neither still could he cause the sudden death of any man. During the time spanning the performance of his vow, the Nazarite is holy. However, failure to uphold any of these ordinances results in the consecration of his head being defiled, which is sin. Then, he must undergo ceremonial cleansing, with his head being shaved on the seventh day, and re-hallowed on the eighth day. This is the ordinance for the man who is not foreordained by God to be a Nazarite but desires to function in that office, as borne out by Scripture.

> And the Lord spake unto Moses, saying, Speak unto the children of Israel, and say unto them, when either man or woman shall separate themselves to vow a vow of a Nazarite, to separate themselves unto the Lord: He shall separate himself from wine and strong drink, and shall drink no vinegar of wine or

vinegar of strong drink, neither shall he drink any liquor of grapes, nor eat moist grapes or dried. All the days of his separation shall he eat nothing that is made of the vine tree, from the kernels, even to the husk. All the days of the vow of his separation there shall no razor come upon his head: until the days be fulfilled in the which he separated himself unto the Lord, he shall be holy and shall let the locks of the hair of his head grow. All the days that he separateth himself unto the Lord he shall come at no dead body. He shall not make himself unclean for his father or his mother, for his brother, or for his sister when they die: because the consecration of his God is upon his head. All the days of his separation he is holy unto the Lord. And if any man die very suddenly by him, and he hath defiled the head of his consecration: then he shall shave his head in the day of his cleansing, on the seventh day shall he shave it. And on the eighth day he shall bring two turtles, or two young pigeons, to the priest, to the door of the tabernacle of the congregation: And the priest shall offer the one for a sin offering, and the other for a burnt offering, and make an atonement for him, for that he sinned by the dead, and shall hallow his head that same day. And he shall consecrate unto the Lord the days of his separation, and shall bring a lamb of the first year for a trespass offering: but the days that were before shall be lost, because his separation was defiled.

Numbers 6:1–12

We observe that despite the three main qualifiers necessary for one to be appointed to the office of the Nazarite by a priest of God, only one was required of Shimshon when God foreordained him. And that was not to allow the hair of his head to be shaven. Shimshon was faithful in obeying this one charge for forty years, until the time appointed to perform the last event necessary to conclude his mission. Even that seeming act of weakness, revealing his secret to Delilah, was an orchestrated act of obeisance to the divine will. Like in a game of chess, this last move lured the adversary to pounce on the bait and become snared in the trap for checkmate! At that point, the partially open doorway of deliverance became the fully open gateway to salvation. This provides still more evidence of Shimshon's unfailing obedience to the Lord.

Another Nazarite of note, Shmu'el (Samuel), in a rebuke to King Saul, said, "Behold, to obey is better than sacrifice, and to hearken than the fat of rams" (1 Samuel 15:22). Out of zeal to obey the word of God when Saul failed to do so, this same Nazarite then slew Agag, king of the Amalekites, before the Lord in Gilgal and dismembered his body. Although, the ordinance of the Nazarite declares that the Nazarite has defiled the head of his consecration when a man dies "very suddenly" by him, yet "Blessed is he whose transgression is forgiven, whose sin is covered. Blessed is the man unto whom the Lord imputeth not iniquity, and in whose spirit there is no guile" (Psalm 32:1–2). Shmu'el was guiltless in this matter and therefore was not required to atone for sin by undergoing the ceremonial cleansing and shaving of his head. He, like Shimshon, remained a Nazarite (holy) until his death.

Summarizing the Mission

We have seen how during the days of his life on earth, Shimshon walked in absolute obedience to the divine purpose, for the Lord's hand was upon him, orchestrating every act according to his plan. From the womb to the day he died, there would be no letup, for he was appointed to be a Nazarite unto God from the womb. Therefore, the Lord began to move him from early on, teaching him obedience, even unto death.

In order to maintain one's consecration, the Nazarite must remain holy before the Lord. We have seen that the Lord maintained Shimshon's sanctification, and how that at the appointed time, he departed from him for a little while so that the stage could be set for his greatest and last campaign on earth: to be the serpent that bites the horse's heel so that the rider falls backward. The Philistine leadership was totally decimated so that Israel enjoyed freedom from oppression for the purpose of organizing themselves spiritually into one nation under God.

This was the singular and long-term purpose for Shimshon's calling, "To begin to deliver Israel from out of the hand of the Philistines." In the aftermath of Shimshon's work, we can see how righteousness got a foothold in the land and spurred spiritual and national unity among the people. An ongoing study through the rest of the book of Judges and continuing through the books of Rut (Ruth) and Shmu'el (Samuel) will not only support but also confirm this.

For starters, in the chapters immediately following the history of Shimshon, we observe the depth of spiritual depravity to which Israel had sunk. Idolatry, anarchy, and sexual uncleanness (including adultery and sodomy) were rampant throughout Israel. Because there was no king, every man did what was right in his own eyes.

Despite the seeming utter profligacy of his people, the Lord began to stoke the smothering coals of righteousness in the heart of Israel. Some Israelites began to hire their own Levite priest to teach them the laws of God, and all Israel united in battle against the unrepentant tribe of Binyamin (Benjamin) to punish them for their sins.

Next, we see the leadership of Israel transitioning

from the judge to the priest (e.g., Eli), to the prophet (e.g., Shmu'el), and finally to the king (e.g., David, etc.). All the while, there was a parallel spiritual growth to the political. Needless to say, spiritual and political order began to be imposed on the people of God and this led to national unity.

Refuting the Allegations

By this time, you should see that all allegations made against Shimshon have no basis on which to stand. These allegations would summarily be thrown out in a court of law. Nevertheless, this book cannot be closed without responding directly to the allegations in chapter one. We must now turn our attention to answering the charges that have been brought against Shimshon down through the ages.

Charge number one: A Nazarite is forbidden to drink wine or strong drink, or to eat anything from the vine. The defendant, Shimshon, did indeed imbibe.

Response number one: This charge is circumstantial at best. Yes, the defendant visited a vineyard where he may have eaten grapes and was married in a traditional ceremony where merrymaking and drinking wine were par for the event. However, the Bible does not specifically mention this; neither does it suggest that Delilah used strong drink as an aid to induce sleep upon Shimshon in order to shave his head. Certainly, we know that the condition—not to drink wine or strong drink—must be met by one who makes the vow of a Nazarite. We also know that Shimshon did not make any vow, but God appointed him. And God, who appointed him, only said that no razor should come upon his head. Therefore, unlike the ordinary Nazarite, Shimshon was not forbidden to refrain from drinking wine or strong drink; he was only required never to allow a razor to come upon his head.

Verdict: Guiltless!

Charge number two: A Nazarite is forbidden to eat any unclean thing. The defendant took and ate honey from the carcass of a lion.

Response number two: Actually, the Nazarite is not exclusively forbidden from eating the unclean thing. Generally, the people of God, of which the Nazarite is a subset, are forbidden from eating the unclean thing, even as Shimshon's mother was forbidden (while he was in the womb to the time he was weaned). Taking into account the special nature of Shimshon's mission—a lone warrior—it is understandable why the Lord imposed only the one condition. Shimshon did not have a following of helpers, cooks, etc., who could furnish a steady or regular supply of sustenance. Nevertheless, it is impossible for Shimshon to violate a condition which he was not required to fulfill.

Verdict: Guiltless!

Charge number three: A Nazarite is forbidden from touching any dead thing. The defendant slew a lion with his bare hands, and then ate honey from its carcass. Besides, many Philistines died suddenly at his hands. Therefore, he defiled his consecration many times over.

Response number three: Again, another affirmation that this requirement was not conditional upon this lone warrior as it also was not applicable to Shmu'el, else the hair of his head would have been shaved many times over.

Verdict: Guiltless!

Charge number four: The Nazarite must not allow a razor to come upon his head. The defendant revealed this secret to his enemies, thereby aiding them.

Response number four: Even as the hand of the Lord

was upon Shimshon, orchestrating everything according to his plan, so was the act of revealing his secret to Delilah. As Yeshua learned obedience unto death, so did Shimshon. At the appointed time, Yeshua said, "My soul is exceeding sorrowful unto death," whereas, in like manner, Shimshon's soul was vexed unto death. Only during the moment when God turned his face away from either of these men could man's will prevail over them. Therefore, it was obedience to God's will and purpose that moved Shimshon to reveal his secret to Delilah. How else would all of the Philistine government be incapacitated in one act? In short, it was necessary that he revealed his secret in order that the divine trap could be sprung.

Verdict: Guiltless!

Charge number five: The Israelite is commanded never to intermarry with the uncircumcised people who lived among them in the promised land. The defendant took a wife from among the heathen people.

Response number five: Technically, this charge is misdirected and should be brought against Shimshon's parents because God commanded the Israelite parents not to give their daughter in marriage nor take a wife unto their son from among the heathen nations. Shimshon's strong supplication prevailed over his parents' objection and such a marriage was arranged. Yet, by the orchestration of the Lord, Shimshon was moved to marry the Philistine woman, but not to return before all Israel to his father's house with her.

Verdict: Guiltless!

Charge number six: It is commanded, "Thou shalt not commit adultery." The defendant actively engaged in sexual intimacy outside of marriage.

Response number six: Shimshon is cited as being sexually involved outside of marriage in at least two relationships. First, there is the one-night affair with the harlot of Gaza, and then the more involved affair with Delilah, the other Philistine woman whom he loved. Apparently, he lived at length with her as man and wife, albeit outside of marriage. Shimshon, a widower, cannot be guilty of adultery because neither he nor the two Philistine women were married. At least one or the other party must be married in order for such an allegation to have any validity. If the charge is fornication, Shimshon's doings were strategies used by the Lord to vex the Philistines in order to smite them since they enticed Israel with their women and caused the Lord to chastise her.

Verdict: Guiltless!

Charge number seven: Shimshon failed to accomplish his God-given mission.

Response number seven: Shimshon was appointed to be a Nazarite unto God (not to man) and to begin to deliver Israel from out of the hand of the Philistines. This assignment was completed. God was the guarantor of this appointment. Surely that what he had begun in Shimshon he was able to complete.

Verdict: Guiltless!

Under Appeal

While rebuttal to all of the charges are accepted, the jury is troubled, in no small way, by the handling of the fornication issue. Is the defense suggesting that it was God's will for the accused to commit fornication, and therefore he is not guilty; or because God's grace covered his transgression, as it does ours in Christ, so his story pictures how God can still use imperfect vessels like us? The jury requests further clarification.

We must consider charge number six now under appeal because there still remain some who are convinced that Shimshon is guilty of fornication, if nothing else. "Even if God used Shimshon's sexual improprieties to accomplish his purpose, the fact is that sin was committed," they say.

Agreed, fornication or murder is sin. But who charges sin to man's account—man or God? And against whom is sin committed—man or God? In both cases, the answer is God alone. But just like you, were not the Pharisees offended when Yeshua said, "Friend, thy sins are forgiven?" (Luke 5:23). Now, if God did not charge sin to Shimshon (notice that each time a Nazarite sins, he loses holiness and must go through the ritual of starting over again), who will upbraid him? God imputed righteousness to Abram because he believed him; if God chose not to impute iniquity to his prepared vessel (Shimshon) because he fully obeyed, will you then be offended at him or him?

Unearthing a Precedence

Within any legal system, there are what is termed gray areas which the law does not directly address. In deliberating such matters, judges use their judicial acumen to render decisions based upon sound interpretation of the intent of the law. Such decisions become precedents upon which subsequent judgments are made in similar or same type cases until the law can directly address the issue or unless that judgment is overturned on appeal by a higher court.

For example, according to the statutes given unto Moshe (Moses) from God with respect to the governance of his people, the inheritance of a father, in Israel, was passed on to his sons only. The law made no provision for daughters. Nevertheless, Numbers 27 recounts how the daughters of Zelophehad petitioned Moshe concerning their claim to their father's right to property in Israel, even though he fathered no sons.

Moshe then consulted God, the author of the law, who ruled in favor of the daughters of Zelophehad. Furthermore, he immediately instructed Moshe to add this new ruling to the statutes on inheritance for future reference. Thereafter, any case involving inheritance could be clarified without resorting to interpreting the intent of the law because it covered both genders.

Similarly, we find indirect precedence in Scripture for the case of Shimshon and the harlot of Gaza, in Genesis 38. Shimshon, a widower at the time of this incident, was a Nazarite unto God, before and after the alleged act of fornication. He retained the same good standing with God after the incident as he had before. This fact must be stated emphatically! Had Shimshon sinned and defiled his consecration, the Holy Spirit would have departed from him, leaving him to shave his head and undergo the rigors described in Numbers 6.

In Genesis 38, we discover that Y'hudah (Judah), progenitor of the tribe of Y'hudah, co-heir of the birthright inheritance with his brother Yosef (Joseph), and like Shimshon, a widower at the time, went in unto a harlot as he traveled along the path to Timnath. Although it turns out that this was no harlot, for all intents and purposes—just as Avraham (Abraham) slew his only son Yitzchak (Isaac) in a figure—Y'hudah committed fornication with a harlot. .

Yet, we know of no punishment being levied upon Y'hudah for this sin or for his complicity in selling his brother to the Ishmaelites. Instead, we know that to his credit, one offspring of this union with the harlot, Phares, is mentioned among the lineage of Yeshua ha Mashiach. We also know that selling Yosef to the Ishmaelites was among the intricate steps in the maze God wrought to save his people in Egypt. How unsearchable is his wisdom! Therefore, like Shmu'el and Shimshon, God blessed Y'hudah instead.

Similarly, we know that Shimshon did nothing of his own accord, but he was constantly moved by the Spirit of God as he sought occasions against the Philistines. Immediately following his incident with the harlot in Gaza, the Holy Spirit of God enabled Shimshon to render the Philistines vulnerable, even as he prophesied against Nineveh in Nahum 3:13 and said, "Behold thy people in the midst of thee are women: the gates of thy land shall be set wide open unto thine enemies: the fire shall devour thy bars." Shimshon performed a monumental task by removing the gates, posts, and bars of the city of Gaza to a location many miles away and leaving them exposed to the mercy of their enemies.

Now, do we use the similar matter of Y'hudah and the harlot to justify Shimshon in the incident with the harlot of Gaza? No! This is used to illustrate that our great and righteous God, who is no respecter of persons, can be, is, and will be, selective about which vessels of his are chosen and used for what purpose. And he alone can and will require, or forgive, sin, and, better yet, not impute sin.

Law of Conquest

But, by a more direct route, we can show that the guiltless verdict rendered in favor of Shimshon is without question the only proper one. In setting up the defense argument for this appeal procedure, we declare beforehand the Scripture reference upon which the defense of this mighty man of faith rests, as Deuteronomy 20:10–14. Next, we clearly state that the accused is a one-man militia deliverer of his people, Israel. As such, he is subject to military protocol. For the one who appointed him said that he would spend the days of his life in service to him alone, and that the only objective of his service was simply to begin the deliverance of Israel from under the oppression of the Philistines.

The accused has admirably and honorably fulfilled his servitude faithfully. From a child, he learned absolute obedience and split-second response to the prodding and quickening of his Master within his spirit.

When he was led in his spirit to marry a Philistine woman, he gave his parents no respite until the matter was accomplished. Needless to say, his master acknowledged, after his demise, that *he* orchestrated all of his servant's deeds. In fact, because the marriage was a military ploy to arrange a sortie against the enemy, it was pointless to continue in it once the objective had been achieved. Therefore, the accused was led in his spirit to forsake the object of his passion and return to his father's house in righteous obedience under his Master's directive.

After the first sortie, the accused was again led in his spirit to take spoil of the enemy immediately following the conquest—which thing is mandated for the man of war. As a solitary militia, this is a military protocol he was apt to learn and continue during his service. His interest for spoil at that time was thirty changes of garment that he relieved his Philistine victims of.

After he had made a conquest of them at Ramath Lehi, he was again led in his spirit into Gaza of the Philistines to take spoil of the enemy. This time, his choice for spoil was a Philistine harlot for whom he had earned every right. Understandably, the Philistine military chafed under the affront of having one of their women being openly and disreputably used by none other than one of the hated, lowly, Hebrews, whose country was in servitude to them. Hence, they set out to ambush and kill this unwary servant of God.

But God, being infinitely more faithful than his servant could ever be, alerted him to the danger surrounding him and enabled him to vanquish them once again. Furthermore, he was empowered to tear apart the protective gate system that helped keep them safe from their enemies.

Following this latest conquest, he ventured into Sorek and took spoil of another Philistine woman whom he kept for himself because he loved her. Once again, being offended by a lowly Hebrew slave cohabitating with another of their women right in the midst of them was unbearable. Lured by the easy proximity to their hated enemy, the Philistine leaders colluded with this man's lover to betray him into their hands. Nevertheless, their wicked scheme was caught up in God's greater stratagem to use his servant to begin delivering his people from under Philistine oppression.

Here now is testament of the ordinance governing the conduct of the military, as it pertains to taking spoil after the conquest. He was commanded to take spoil of his enemy.

> When thou comest nigh unto a city to fight against it, then proclaim peace unto it. And it shall be, if it make answer of peace, and open unto thee, then it shall be, that all the people that is found therein shall be tributaries unto thee, and they shall serve thee. And if it will make no peace with thee, but will make war against thee, then thou shalt besiege it. And when the Lord thy God hath delivered it into thine hands, thou shalt smite every male thereof with the edge of the sword: But the women, and the little ones, and the cattle, and all that is in the city, even all the spoil thereof, shalt thou take unto thyself; and thou shalt eat the spoil of thine enemies, which the Lord thy God hath given thee.
>
> Deuteronomy 20:10–14

Again, we repeat that the overriding virtue in Shimshon's appointment is his unbroken service as a Nazarite, regardless of the specific acts he carried out. Therefore, the guiding factor in studying the acts of Shimshon must be rooted in total acceptance of his calling as a Nazarite. You must accept that his sexual activities were not lustful escapades, but were fully orchestrated by the Holy Spirit in total accord with Scripture. As a lifelong Nazarite unto God, he was diligent and faithful in service. Shimshon's commission was strictly a militia operation with the Lord probing the enemy to find occasions which could be used to set up confrontations. Each triumph entitled him to his choice of the spoil according to the law of conquest. It is evident that the Philistine woman was a sore spot for this proud nation, or the Lord would not have used the same strategy so successfully over and over. Herewith, the defense rests.

The Litmus Test

The Nazarite vow is the best (no, the only) indicator of proof as to whether Shimshon was guilty of sin or not. Numbers 6:8 reads, "All the days of his separation he is holy unto the Lord." Therefore, any un-holiness or defilement of the head of his consecration is sin, for which he must be shaven, etc. Now, how many times was Shimshon shaven?

The answer is once. Therefore, the number of times that sin was imputed to him was one time only! (That being the moment he acquiesced to death when he revealed the source of his strength to Delilah.)

Psalm 32:1–2

"Blessed is he whose transgression is forgiven, whose sin is *covered*. Blessed is the man unto whom the Lord imputeth not iniquity, and in whose spirit there is no guile."

Notice that Scripture does not say, "Blessed is the man whose sin is blotted out," but "whose sin is covered." The Hebrew word for *blot* or *blotted* means "to erase or rub off." The inference being, that a mark or stain upon an object must be treated one way or another in order to remove or expunge it. On the other hand, the Hebrew root *kacah,* which is properly translated as "covered," and its derivative *keceh,* which means "fullness, appointed; infer an object that is fully covered for a time appointed." The implication here is that an object is fully shielded so that no mark or stain can affix itself to the surface of the object for as long as it is covered. Therefore, the object remains mar-less; not because of cleansing, but because it is protected from being marred. Hence, the "guiltless" verdict in favor of Shimshon.

"This is the Lord's doing; it is marvelous in our eyes" (Psalm 118:23). Sin could not affix itself to Shimshon because he was totally covered by the Holy Spirit, and our God is a consuming fire.[44] In chapter six of this book, we learned that once sanctified, the altar is most holy and that anything touching it becomes holy. Furthermore, God (Yeshua) asked, which is greater—the gift (Shimshon) or the altar that sanctifies the gift? Would not the altar, the Holy Spirit, consume any sin? His covering is why sin could not affix itself to him, and none could be imputed to him either.

Thus, it pleased God to empower Shimshon to total obedience under the anointing of the Holy Spirit (as Yeshua was driven into the wilderness so was Shimshon driven to complete obedience) according to the prearranged terms of Psalm 32:1–2. That is, he was cloaked in a robe of holiness to the Lord from the womb, and his cloak was the Holy Spirit.

Just so you are not left with the impression that this blessedness was reserved to Shimshon alone, let's take a look at how another expounds on this passage. The apostle Shaul (Paul) says, "Blessed are they whose iniquities are forgiven, and whose sins are covered" (Romans 4:7). By this, we know that they (the sons of God) are many whose iniquities are forgiven and whose sins are covered so long as they abide in Mashiach (Messiah) and his word abide in them.

Guilty vs. Not-Guilty vs. Guiltless

A guilty verdict infers that one had been justifiably charged; a not-guilty verdict infers that one may have been wrongly charged, though the possibility exists that in the face of strong evidence the accused might have been convicted; a guiltless verdict emphasizes absolute freedom from guilt. Consequently, a guilty verdict for Shimshon is out of hand as is a "not guilty" one. The only possible verdict is guiltless to the charges as proved by the litmus test.

Finally, as Yeshua was sinless because he committed no sin, so was Shimshon guiltless of sin because of his select status. However, each man obediently became sin in order for the divine plan of salvation to unfold.

Conclusion

In concluding the matter pertaining to the alleged sins or faults of Shimshon, we assert that not one allegation has any merit in light of the truths that have been revealed within these pages. For more than three thousand years since Shimshon died, the truth about his calling and mission here on earth has been misinterpreted, misunderstood, and misrepresented in, to, and amongst the Jewish and Christian communities.

Not only is it high time for these truths to be revealed so that this servant of God can receive the rightful honor due a faithful servant, but also that every believer can grow in faith, and that in all this, God can be glorified. One can only marvel at the intricacies wrought by the Lord in weaving such a maze for his enemies through Shimshon. Everything he did through Shimshon was open and righteous, for there is no shadow of turning with the Lord. From the enacting of the Avrahamic covenant and continuing through the penetration of his army onto the beachhead that was the promised land, Jehovah Sabbaoth had every legal right to advance his kingdom throughout the entire earth.

Undoubtedly, Shimshon proved to be a rather effective arrow out of God's quiver, not only by what he accomplished, but also by the ongoing effects since. The doorway of salvation was opened to national Israel, the root and subset of God's people on the earth first, so that the work begun by Shimshon could be completed in Yeshua and offered even to them who before knew not God as God.

Therefore, it pleased the Lord to honor Shimshon by mentioning him among the notable servants of faith in Hebrews 11. And now we understand why—Shimshon was also a blessed man unto whom the Lord would not impute iniquity, and in whose spirit was found no guile.

TYPOLOGY

Call for the Neo-Nazarite

Shimshon and the Philistines of his time have long since passed away from the face of the earth, but the very same Spirit that moved him at times now indwells every believer all over the earth today. That same old spirit of the Philistines who bedeviled all Israel to cause them to turn away from the Lord and be enticed to sin in order that his anger should be kindled against them is just as wily, as subtle, and as active as ever in the world. This worldly spirit is the character and persona of the devil, the serpent that beguiled Eve in the garden.

In the presence of such an unrelenting, wicked foe, the Lord has equipped each believer, lest we fall, with his Holy Spirit, who in us is greater than that one who is in the world. If we will avail ourselves under his power, "He is able to do exceedingly abundantly above all we can ask or think" so that all the world might know that there is one God, and that he, Yeshua ha Mashiach, is Lord.

In these last days that precede and bring us into the end-time tribulation period, it is written that men will be lovers of self, deceivers, breakers of covenants, and you name it. They will become utterly depraved spiritually. They will rise to call good evil, and evil good, reversing the order of godliness. In fact, while they wax bold and strong in their attempt to snuff out the truth of God's Word, the just will suffer persecution and even death.[45]

This will be reminiscent of the period of the judges of Israel when every man did what was right in his own eyes instead of doing what was right in the sight of God. In preparation for this, God is looking for the Nazarites of our time who will favor Israel, his righteous cause, through whom he can continually validate his presence in the world, who will keep men mindful of his enduring truth and require righteousness both of men and nations. This is the call of the neo-Nazarite. Will you opt to be a Nazarite unto God?

Similarities and Contrasts

The current chapter of this work draws your attention to the remarkable similarities and contrasts between the life, mission, and characteristics of Yeshua ha Mashiach and Shimshon. The life, ministry, and death of Shimshon foreshadow that of the Lord, Yeshua ha Mashiach, in much too many ways to be coincidental. If so, then the happenstances are uncanny. This work makes a strong case that the man, Shimshon, is a type of Yeshua; that he came in the spirit of the very same angel of the Lord, whose name is Wonderful, who performed wonderously in the presence of Manoah and his wife.

Table of Similarities and Contrasts

Shimshon	Characteristic	Yeshua
Judges 13:3, 5–Thou shalt conceive and bear a son; he shall be a Nazarite unto God from the womb, and shall begin to deliver Israel from under the Philistines.	Birth and Mission foretold Deliverer/Saver Began/Completed	Matthew 1:21–She shall bring forth a son, and you shall call his name Yeshua; for he shall save his people from their sins. John 19:30–It is finished.
Genesis 49:16–Dan (Shimshon) shall judge (rule, contend for, minister/execute judgment) his people. Judges 15:20–He judged Israel twenty years.	Judge vs Grace	John 1:17–Grace and truth came by him. John 3:17–God sent not his son into the world to condemn it; but that through him it might be saved.
Judges 16:16–His soul was vexed unto death. Judges 16:30–Let me die with the Philistines.	The Vicarious One Obedient unto Death	Mark 14:34–My soul is exceeding sorrowful unto death. Philippians 2:8–He humbled himself and became obedient unto death.
Scripture records none.	Posterity	Isaiah 53:9–Who shall declare his generation?

Judges 16:18–Then the lords of the Philistines came to Delilah, whom he loved, with money in their hands.	Betrayed by Bosom Friend	Matthew 26:15–And they covenanted with Judas for 30 pieces of silver. Psalm 41:9–My own friend has lifted up his heel against me.
Judges 16:25–And they called for Shimshon to make them sport.	Was Mocked and Scorned	Psalm 22:7–They all laugh me to scorn. Luke 22:63–And the men that held Yeshua mocked him.
Deuteronomy 33:22–Dan (Shimshon) is a lion's whelp.	Lion	Revelation 5:5–Behold, the Lion of the tribe of Juda hath prevailed.
Judges 14:12–19 - Honored his word to give a change of garment to each of his companions despite their dishonesty.	Honor his word	Psalm 138:2–Has magnified his word above his name. Hebrews 7:25–Liveth evermore to make intercession for all who believe.
Judges 16:24 - Enemy and destroyer of the Philistines.	Destroyer	1 John 3:8 Manifested to destroy the works of the devil. Acts 10:38 went about doing good and healing all that were oppressed by the devil.

Judges 14:2–I have seen a woman of the Philistines: now get her for me to wife. Judges 14:3–Is there never a woman among thy brethren that thou goest to take a wife of the Philistines?	Ventured out among a foreign people to choose a bride unto himself	Revelation 9:7–8–Marriage of the Lamb has come, whose wife is the saints.
Hebrews 11:2, 32–34–Through faith he subdued a kingdom, wrought righteousness, obtained promises, stopped the mouth of a lion, etc. and obtained a good report.	Faithful	Revelation 3:14–The faithful and true witness. 1 Thessalonians 5:24–Faithful is he who called, and to do all that he promised Hebrews 10:23–For he is faithful that promised. .
Judges 16:5–Entice him, and see wherein his great strength lieth . . .	Mighty One	Isaiah 9:6–His name shall be called The Mighty God.
Judges 16:16–His soul was vexed unto death. Numbers 6:8–All the days of his separation he is holy. Judges 16:30–Shimshon called to the Lord and said, "Let me die with the Philistines."	Became Sin/ Was smitten	Matthew 26:38–His soul was exceeding sorrowful unto death. 2 Corinthians 5:21–Became sin for us even though himself was sinless. Isaiah 53:4– Smitten of God and afflicted for our sakes.

Judges 16:17–If I be shaven, then my strength will go from me, and I shall become weak . . . ie become appointed to affliction . . . and be like any other man.	From Invincibility to appointment with Affliction	Isaiah 53:10–Yet it pleased the Lord to bruise him; he hath put him to grief . . . ie appointed him to affliction . . .
Judges 16:30–He slew more at his death than in his lifetime.	Accomplished more in death	John 12:24–Except a kernel of wheat falls into the ground and dies, it abides alone: but if it dies, it brings forth even more.
Genesis 49:16– Dan shall be a serpent in the way; an adder in the path that biteth the horse heels, so that his rider shall fall backward.	Serpent Destroyer Vs. Serpent Healer	Numbers 21:9 - If a serpent had bitten any man when he beheld the serpent of brass, he lived. John 12:32–And I, if I be lifted up from the earth, I will draw all men unto me. John 3:14, 15–And as Moses lifted up the serpent . . . so must the Son of man be lifted up: That whosoever believeth in him shall not perish but have eternal life.

Judges 15:13–And they bound him with two new cords and brought him up from the rock	Bound and Delivered by kinsmen to enemies	Mark 15:1 - And binding Jesus, they led him away, and delivered him up to Pilate.

Hebrews 12:1, 2–Wherefore seeing we also are compassed about with so great a cloud of witnesses, let us lay aside every weight, and the sin which doth so easily beset us, and let us run with patience the race that is set before us, looking unto Jesus the author and finisher of our faith; who for the joy that was set before him endured the cross, despising the shame, and is set down at the right hand of the throne of God.

Shimshon's leg of the race was to begin to deliver God's people from bondage so that the beachhead of salvation for Israel could be established and spread to the Gentiles.	Beginner & Finisher of God's Salvation Relay Team	Yeshua is the Anchor leg for God's Salvation Relay Team. What Shimshon began was finished in him, and by him on the cross. Therefore all Israel will be saved.

ISRAEL AND THE GENTILE CHURCH

Another Type

Through Shimshon, we are provided with a glorious enactment of God's gift of perfect remission from sins. His story presents us with a picture of God pouring the fullness of his wrath and vengeance upon them that hate him and his unlimited mercy, forgiveness, and compassion upon them who love him. The work begun by Shimshon as he contended for the house of Ya'akov (Jacob) points to the work accomplished by Yeshua on the cross for Israel and the Gentile nations. He was a precursor to Yeshua.

For example, the Philistine nation was a prime recipient of God's wrath and vengeance over a period from the time of the judges to the time of King Hezekiah. They were among Israel's most relentless and merciless foes. Because of their tremendous pride and continued wickedness, God vowed that the remnant of the Philistines would perish.[46] Today, after drinking from the wine cup of his fury, the Philistines no longer exist as a people.

On the other hand, God is unlimited in bestowing

mercy, forgiveness, and compassion upon all who love him and keep his commandments. Israel, during the period of the judges and forevermore, is a prime example of this. He chastised them when they transgressed his laws, but he delivered them when they cried out for mercy, over and over again, even devising ingenuous plans of deliverance such as with Shimshon. Today, Israel is re-established as a nation in the land of Canaan.

According to the manner of man, Shimshon's life was a parody of his calling to be a Nazarite. He, seemingly, did not try to uphold the conditions necessary to continue as one. Through the ages, men have struggled to explain why God continued to perform mightily through such a "flawed" vessel. Despite the clamor for over three thousand years concerning Shimshon's sin-laden life, this manuscript has carefully declared his guiltlessness, never asserting that he did not commit sinful acts, but that sin was never imputed to him. There is obvious irony wherein a man called into an exemplary office of holiness, not only fails to uphold its dictates, but also contrarily, continues to perform wonderful works without having to remedy his ways. Although the gifts and calling of God are without repentance,[47] the Lord is far (removed) from the wicked.[48] Therefore, if Shimshon was impious, the Lord's presence would not have lingered with or upon him forever. How then can God's continued presence with Shimshon be explained, except by the revelation God has given us through his Word?

Shimshon remained guiltless because he was fully shielded from sin by the Holy Spirit, who is a consuming fire and the sanctifier. His transgressions were consumed away by the fire of the Lord; his iniquities were not imputed to him because the thoughts and desires of his heart were orchestrated by the Lord continuously. If you will receive it, Shimshon's triumphs benefited the house of Ya'akov directly, and his blessing has been held in store for them for a season yet to come. More directly, all Israel, in the season from the resurrection of Yeshua to his return, will be saved by the mercies of God. He was Israel's champion. He triumphed so that their spiritual eyes would be opened, and that the beachhead of salvation would be established for them and extended to the Gentiles through Yeshua. Transgression and iniquity were remitted to him before remission was preached to man by Yeshua ha Mashiach (which in itself is a foreshadowing). This pardon or blessing which tolerated sin by Shimshon has been held in reserve for God's elect from Shimshon, their champion. Precisely because God, in his infinite wisdom, knowing that Israel, after suffering spiritual blindness in order that all Gentiles might enter into his kingdom, would have no chance to salvation if left to the same Gentiles, "... hath concluded them all in unbelief, that he might have mercy upon all" (Romans 11:32): Unbelief to Israel because they received not their Mashiach; unbelief to the Gentiles because they were unmerciful to their fellow servants.

If this blessing that tolerates sin was laid upon Israel through Shimshon for a season, then remission of sins came to Israel as well as to the Gentiles through Yeshua for this season. This became necessary in order that those who were blinded for the sake of the Gentiles entering in might not perish. But for those of the household of Ya'akov who, along with the Gentiles, have been fortunate to receive salvation at this time, a different, but equal, mechanism is made available to all through faith in Yeshua, whereby remission of sins can be accessed on an ongoing basis, "If we confess our sins, he is faithful and just to forgive us our sins, and to cleanse us from all unrighteousness" (1 John 1:9). This is parity, for God is not a respecter of persons. The same benefit given to God's elect through Shimshon's portrayal has been accorded to both Israel and the Gentiles through faith in Yeshua.

Now, we must treat the doctrine of remission of sins as it impacts Scripture before the first advent of Yeshua ha Mashiach. Before commencing his ministry, there is no mention of remission of sins in Scripture. The basis for any new covenant doctrine must be rooted in prior old covenant teaching. And, although no direct old covenant passage taught this doctrine, the Lord was not lax to give us an example for the remission of sins in the Torah (book of the law and prophets).

The word remission, translated from the Greek aphesis, means "freedom, to pardon, put away, to let, tolerate, etc." We know that remission of sins is available to all believers through the blood of Yeshua for all past sins.[49] We also know that without repentance, there can be no remission of sins. Because the penalty for past sins was impossible for man to pay and still live, God relaxed it by granting him freedom from the requirement of the law, by taking upon himself the payment for sin. The law cannot be broken (before one jot or tittle of the law can pass away, heaven and earth would have to pass away) without the price being paid.

In Shimshon's life, we see a depiction of the coming remission of sins for God's elect. First of all, the angel of the Lord prophesied that Shimshon would be a Nazarite unto God from conception to death. We know that man has a sin nature, "For all have sinned and come short of the glory of God" (Romans 3:23). Therefore, no man by himself can remain holy unto God without violating that holiness. Still, the Nazarite must remain holy unto God during the entire period of his separation. For Shimshon, this meant unbroken holiness throughout his lifetime. As impossible as it is for a spiritually mature person to maintain himself in this manner, how much harder would it be for a child? We know that Shimshon remained a Nazarite throughout his childhood, even though Scripture rightly says that foolishness (ungodliness) is bound in the heart of a child. Yet, no guile was found in his heart, for we have shown that there was integrity between the word in his heart being affirmed by what he said and did (see chapter six). Therefore, something out of the ordinary was necessary to maintain his holiness. This extraordinary something shielded Shimshon from sin and guile.

As the contender for and champion of the house of Ya'akov, all that was Shimshon's became Israel's in the same manner that the blessings of Avraham (Abraham) are handed down to all believers because he is the father of faith to all who believe. Similarly, the blessing of Shimshon is held in abeyance for Israel until the house of Ya'akov (Jacob) is transformed. The Holy Spirit is the unconditional cover from sin for Ya'akov as depicted by Shimshon, and Yeshua is the cover from sin for Israel and the Church through the righteousness of faith. With his death on the cross, Yeshua satisfied the requirement of the law for all time for all who repent and believe. Through faith in Yeshua, the spirit of man abides in Yeshua, and his words abide in the heart of man. Thus, we have parallelism between Shimshon abiding under the cloak of the Holy Spirit and the spirit of the new covenant believer abiding in Yeshua, with one significant difference.

Although both are essentially covered from the penalty of sin, Shimshon was pre-pardoned from conception to death from all sins, not just the penalty thereof; whereas, the believer is pardoned from all past sins, empowered to live unto righteousness, and continues to enjoy pardon from sin if he will continue to confess his sins. Herein, we notice a peculiar application of remission of sins toward Shimshon. The reason for this difference lies in the fact that the heart or spirit of Shimshon was completely under the control of God at all times, in that he bore the consecration of God upon his head from conception. Ordinarily, the believer cannot be completely controlled by God because he is not consecrated unto God. (By way of illustration, there are three types of the Christian: the believer of the Word can be likened to man's developmental stages spanning childhood through adolescence, indiscipline characterizes him; the disciple of the Word can be likened to man's developmental stage spanning mature adulthood, energy and discipline are his hallmarks; and the apostle of the Word can be likened to man's developmental stage spanning old age, diminished physical attributes, discipline, and complete reliance on God, as when Ya'akov became Israel, sets him apart. That is why the Lord commissioned the Church to make disciples of all nations: obedience of this command would assure an unbroken supply of vessels, Jew or Gentile, prepared for his work).

During this period of the Church Age, Israel has suffered spiritual blindness in order that other sheep of Gentile nations should be brought into the kingdom of heaven. This, in itself, by no means prohibits co-entry to the Jews at this time. On the contrary, God requires that by mercy, Gentiles should provoke them to jealousy, meaning that they would then diligently desire that which the Gentiles have attained, which thing was previously theirs. And Shaul asks, wistfully, "If their temporary fall results in riches to the Gentiles, can you imagine the impact of the fullness of their inclusion in the Church?"[50] Because the Church has neglected to show love to Israel in order that they are provoked to jealousy, the Lord promises to return to Jerusalem with mercies.

The Mercies of God

In that day, the armies of the world will be gathered against Jerusalem[51] and suddenly there shall appear the deliverer out of Zion who will take away ungodliness from Ya'akov (Jacob).[52] Then all Israel shall be saved. Please note the distinction: Ya'akov includes the impenitent, as well as penitent Jew, whereas Israel is the repentant Jew. As Ya'akov became Israel when he yielded to God, so too will all Israel be saved when ungodliness is removed from Ya'akov.

If your question is "Why would God arbitrarily act to save Ya'akov (Israel)?" remember that God is never arbitrary. Instead, his Word is law and cannot be broken. Since he has said, "And he shall reign over the house of Ya'akov for ever" (Luke 1:33), then thus it must be. Finally, due to the Church's lack of mercy toward Ya'akov, it becomes necessary for God to intervene in order for the same salvation to be extended to Israel. For he said, "As concerning the gospel, they are enemies for your sakes: but as touching the election, they are beloved for the fathers' sakes. For the gifts and calling of God are without repentance" (Romans 11:28–29). Therefore, "God hath concluded them (including us) all in unbelief, that he might have mercy upon all" (Romans 11:32). So, if there is enmity between Jew and Gentile because of the gospel, we still have no excuse for not loving them: for he says, "Love your enemies ... pray for them who despitefully use you" (Matthew 5:44). God is not arbitrary but faithful. This end-time salvation of Israel is not arbitrary. It was foreshadowed, being symbolized in the re-consecration of Shimshon's head. But listen to what God has said concerning Ya'akov and Israel:

But now thus saith the Lord that created thee, O Jacob, and he that formed thee, O Israel, Fear not: for I have redeemed thee, I have called thee by thy name; thou art mine. When thou passest through the waters, I will be with thee; and through the rivers, they shall not overflow thee: when thou walkest through the fire, thou shalt not be burned; neither shall the flame kindle upon thee. For I am the Lord thy God, the Holy One of Israel, thy Savior: I gave Egypt for thy ransom, Ethiopia and Seba for thee. Since thou wast precious in my sight, thou hast been honorable, and I have loved thee: therefore will I give men for thee, and people for thy life.

Isaiah 43:1–4

Continuing in that same day, God will open up a fountain of cleansing from sin unto Judah and the inhabitants of Jerusalem. And he will pour the spirit of grace and of supplications upon them so that they shall mourn bitterly when they look upon him whom they have pierced, even as they would for their firstborn. Then will one ask him, "What are these wounds in your hands?" And he will answer tenderly, "Wounds which were inflicted in the house of my friends."[53]

While they mourn bitterly for him, he will turn their mourning into joy and cause them to rejoice from their sorrow. For, says he, "I will forgive their iniquity and remember their sin no more. Then God will make a new covenant with Israel."[54] In Micah 7:19, it is written, "He will subdue our inquities; and thou wilt cast all their sins into the depths of the sea." In other words, he destroys their propensity toward sin, thereby eliminating their sin problem forever!

So what happens to Jews who died as Ya'akov after the resurrection but before the second coming? Will they be saved too? The answer is yes, insofar as they believe and receive their Mashiach in the day when they see the piercings. They shall be transformed from Ya'akov to Israel in an instant of belief (faith). "Seeing it is one God which shall justify the circumcision by faith, and the uncircumcision through faith." Did you get that? Yes, Israel is saved by faith, but the Gentiles are saved through faith.[55] As the gospel was preached to the dead before, so will it also be preached to the Jews, who died, having suffered blindness for our sakes without ever receiving mercy in turn from us. "For this cause was the gospel preached also to them that are dead, that they might be judged according to men in the flesh, but live according to God in the spirit" (1 Peter 4:6). We find affirmation for this in Hosea 13:9 and 14. There, while pitying the plight of Israel (that is, all Jews), God gives the following assurance, "O, Israel, thou hast destroyed thyself; but in me is thine help. I will be thy king...I will ransom them from the power of the grave [sheol or hell]; I will redeem them from death [the grave]: O death, I will be thy plagues; O grave, I will be thy destruction: repentance [for hell and the grave] shall be hid from mine eyes."

If you did not know, Shimshon was symbolic of the house of Ya'akov, but even more than that, Yeshua became the embodiment of Israel, God's firstborn. Shimshon's life depicts and foreshadows the way of Ya'akov and God's grace and mercy toward him. At the end of the age, with the eyes of Israel once again blinded to spiritual realities, Shimshon in the person of Yeshua running the anchor leg of salvation, steps up with the blessings of Shimshon that had been held in store for this particular time—that of being pre-pardoned from sins if one only believe. So the serpent that destroys gives way to the serpent that heals. Yeshua depicts the fullness of Israel as the firstborn of God in him. If the Gentiles find this hard to receive, how will they react when Israel, the olive tree, begins once again to blossom and stands ready to receive the blessings of the firstborn? 'For the least shall become preeminent in the kingdom of God.' God did not conceal this but revealed the Church's hardness of heart toward Israel before hand through the parables of the barren fig tree and the evil eye so that we might take heed.

Given to the Nations

The parables below show the gravity of the responsibility God attaches to disseminating the gospel of the kingdom to the lost world. The principal means of accomplishing this is by love: loving God above all and loving our brothers as we do ourselves. This is the fruit of the kingdom, and we are required to bear that fruit abundantly and share it freely. Thus will the world know that we are his and that we are one in him.

> There was a certain householder, who planted a vineyard, and hedged it round about, and digged a winepress in it, and built a tower, and let it out to husbandmen, and went into a far country: and when the time of the fruit drew near, he sent his servants to the husbandmen, that they might receive the fruits of it. And the husbandmen took his servants, and beat one, and killed another, and stoned another. Again, he sent other servants more than the first: and they did unto them likewise. But last of all he sent unto them his son, saying, They will reverence my son. But when the husbandmen saw the son, they said among themselves, This is the heir; come, let us kill him, and let us seize on his inheritance. And they caught him, and cast him out of the vineyard, and slew him. When the lord therefore of the vineyard

cometh, what will he do unto those husbandmen? They say unto him, He will miserably destroy those wicked men, and will let out his vineyard unto other husbandmen, which shall render him the fruits in their seasons. Jesus saith unto them, Did ye never read in the Scriptures, The stone which the builders rejected, the same is become the head of the corner: this is the Lord's doing, and it is marvelous in our eyes? Therefore say I unto you, The Kingdom of God shall be taken from you, and given to a nation bringing forth the fruits thereof.

Matthew 21:33-43

Parable of the Evil Eye

The following prophetic parable is given to show the path taken by the Gentile Church with respect to Israel, beginning after the resurrection of Yeshua and continuing to the end of this age. The challenge still facing the Church is to provoke Jews to jealousy through love, and to turn inactivity into active evangelization of Jews under the able supervision of the Holy Spirit.

> For the kingdom of heaven is like unto a man that is a householder which went out early in the morning to hire laborers into his vineyard. And when he had agreed with the laborers for a penny a day, he sent them into his vineyard. And he went out about the third hour, and saw others standing idle in the marketplace. And he said unto them; Go ye also into the vineyard, and whatsoever is right I will give you. And they went their way. Again he went out about the sixth and ninth hour, and did likewise. And about the eleventh hour he went out, and found others standing idle, and saith unto them, Why stand ye here all the day idle? They say unto him, Because

no man hath hired us. He saith unto them, Go ye also into the vineyard; and whatsoever is right, that shall ye receive. So when even was come, the lord of the vineyard saith unto his steward, Call the laborers, and give them their hire, beginning from the last unto the first. And when they came that were hired about the eleventh hour, they received every man a penny. And when the first came, they supposed that they should have received more; and they murmured against the goodman of the house, saying, These last have wrought but one hour, and thou hast made them equal unto us, which have borne the burden and heat of the day. But he answered one of them, and said, Friend, I do thee no wrong: didst not thou agree with me for a penny? Take that thine is, and go thy way: I will give unto this last, even as unto thee. Is it not lawful for me to do what I will with mine own? *Is thine eye evil, because I am good?* So the last shall be first, and the first last: for many be called, but few chosen.

Matthew 20:1–16

The Foundation

So what do we make of this dark saying, and how is it applicable to us today? According to Isaiah 28:9 and 10, we attain understanding of doctrine by patiently laying precept upon precept upon precept, and line upon line upon line: a little here, then, there a little, until by and large we come into full understanding. Kefa goes further with this and says, "No prophecy of the Scripture is of any private interpretation" (2 Peter 1:20). Therefore, let Scripture be the one and only arbiter of Scripture.

We find a song written in the book of Isaiah that casts some light upon our subject parable:

Now will I sing to my well beloved a song of my beloved touching his vineyard. My well beloved hath a vineyard in a very fruitful hill. And he fenced it, and gathered out the stones thereof, and planted it with the choicest vine, and built a tower in the midst of it, and also made a winepress therein: and he looked that it should bring forth grapes, and it brought forth wild grapes. And now, O inhabitants of Jerusalem, and men of Judah, judge, I pray you, betwixt me and my vineyard: what could have been done more to my vineyard that I have not done in it? Wherefore, when I looked that it should bring forth grapes, brought it forth wild grapes? And now go to; I will tell you what I will do to my vineyard: I will take away the hedge thereof, and it shall be eaten up; and break down the wall thereof, and it shall be trodden down: And I will lay it waste: it shall not be pruned nor digged; but there shall come up briers and thorns: I will also command the clouds that they rain no rain upon it. For the vineyard of the Lord of Hosts is the house of Israel, and the men of Judah, his pleasant plant: and he looked for judgment, but behold oppression; for righteousness, but behold a cry.

Isaiah 5:1–7

Another passage of Scripture sheds more light upon our subject parable, so that we might render a true interpretation:

But when he saw the multitudes, he was moved with compassion on them, because they fainted, and were scattered abroad, as sheep having no shepherd. Then saith he unto his disciples, The harvest truly is plenteous, but the laborers are few; Pray therefore the Lord of the harvest, that he will send forth laborers into his harvest.

Matthew 9:36–38

Still another point of clarification is found in Luke 19:12 and 13. There, Yeshua presents a parable, "A certain nobleman went into a far country to receive for himself a kingdom, and to return. And he called his ten servants, and delivered them ten pounds, and said unto them, Occupy till I come." Which means, "busy yourselves" or "be occupied" with what you have received until my return.

Finally, just what is the nature of this occupation that the servants should be engaged in? Yeshua specifies this in Matthew 28:19. He said, "Go ye therefore, and teach all nations, baptizing them in the name of the Father, and of the Son, and of the Holy Ghost." But in Luke 24:46–47, he is more precise, specifying exactly where they were to begin the work. He said, "Thus it is written, and thus it behooved Christ to suffer, and to rise from the dead the third day: And that repentance and remission of sins should be preached in his name among all nations, beginning at Jerusalem."

Remember that we are laying precept upon precept upon precept, and line upon line upon line. And with patience, we soon will possess full understanding of this body of knowledge.

Identifying Important Elements

In order to understand the parable properly, we must correctly identify the important elements and give meaning to them. But without the foundational passages, we could not fully understand the parable nor identify the elements.

The kingdom of heaven refers to the realm of God's dwelling and its jurisdiction. Its significance rests upon the fact that since the time of Yeshua, the kingdom is present in the earth realm also. First, Yochanan the baptizer, then Yeshua both trumpeted this truth at the start of their ministries by preaching, "Repent, for the Kingdom of Heaven is at hand" (Matthew 3:2; 4:17). Enlarging on this, Yeshua said to his disciples, "Repent, for the Kingdom of Heaven is at hand; heal the sick, cleanse the lepers, cast out devils, etc," which signifies that this kingdom, like any other kingdom, has dominion. It is able to exert its authority and power within and upon its territory. The regenerate human vessel becomes the possession or territory of the kingdom of heaven on earth and the launching point or beachhead from which it can exert and/or expand its authority, power, and influence.[56] Therefore, Yeshua ordered his disciples not only to spread the good news about the kingdom, but also to enforce its authority. No maladies or evils are present or tolerated in heaven; therefore, none should abide within man, the new domain or territory of heaven on earth.

- Man - male or female-born of a woman on earth, thereby possessing legitimate earthly residence.
- Householder - a man who possesses and controls real property on earth. Yeshua is this householder.
- Time - measure of a period of lapse such as a day (multiples or portions thereof–age, year, hours, minutes, seconds), etc. Here, the day refers to this age.
- Laborer - a supervised worker or toiler; one who is occupied by work. The laborers here are the believers. Clergymen first hired, laymen last hired.
- Vineyard - place of cultivation of fruit/food-bearing vines. The nation Israel, comprising the Jews, is God's vineyard. Disciples were to be cultivated in this vineyard.

- Penny/Reward - money or other valuable instrument of exchange. Here, eternal life is rewarded to all who believe in Yeshua and are led by the Spirit of God.
- Steward - a tutor, commissioner, or manager; one who permits or allows. The Holy Spirit is God's steward.
- Evil eye - exhibiting effects or influence of evil (such as thought, envy, greed, etc.,) but not possessing the evil character or being essentially evil.
- Harvest - to reap or gather that which was sown. However, in this age, the harvest consists of planting and watering the Word of God in the heart of man.

Meaning of the Parable

Seeing the condition of and being moved with great compassion toward his vineyard, the Lord diligently hired laborers into the harvest (of the vineyard) from the very beginning, and continued to do so, even at the eleventh hour, before the end of the age. He was keen to negotiate a price with the laborers prior to them commencing work. But having charged all servants to busy themselves with the task at hand, beginning at Jerusalem, he was amazed to find them idle at every turn that he should need to hire them again. He resolved to pay all laborers, even those hired later during the workday, the same as the first hired.

The kingdom of heaven is described here as a man who possesses great real estate, which includes a vineyard. This man is described as a householder, meaning that he exercises direct control over his estate. Not having enough laborers capable to tend the vineyard, he goes outside to hire workers at the first light of day. He strikes a deal with the laborers at a penny for a full day's work. Realizing as time goes by that more laborers are needed for the work in the vineyard, the householder returns repeatedly at the third, sixth, ninth, and eleventh hour and supplements his workforce, being careful to inform them each time that they will be paid what is right. Finally, at the end of the day, he instructs his steward to call the laborers and pay their earnings, beginning from those hired last to the first. So, the steward paid those hired at the eleventh hour one penny per man. He continued paying at this same rate to all the others and to those who were hired first. But those who were first hired figured that they deserved more; therefore, they began to murmur against their benefactor, saying, "Those guys worked for only one hour, whereas we worked throughout the heat of the entire day, and you paid them the same as us?" Therefore, the benefactor said to one of them, "I have been righteous in all of my dealings with you. Is it not my prerogative to do with my resources as I please? Why do you exhibit an evil eye toward me, in spite of my graciousness toward you? Take your portion and go your way." And then, he pronounces a sentence upon them, "You who would be preeminent among your brothers shall be least in the kingdom of heaven; and you who are unassuming among your brothers shall become preeminent."

The Broader Picture

The householder is the Lord, that nobleman who came all the way to earth to receive for himself a kingdom. He is full of compassion for the well-being of Israel, his vineyard. He personally invested three years into planting the choicest vines in a fruitful site. The choice vines are men of Israel, men who receive him with praise and live to celebrate him. At the time of harvest, he expected to reap a crop of choice grapes. But instead, worthless, wild grapes were what he received. Therefore, what should he do concerning his investment? What would you do?

By the end of the first century, when the apostles, the choicest plantings, were deceased, we see the complete excommunication of Jewish believers from the synagogues. We also see the increasing push into leadership of the so-called (Gentile) Church fathers and their growing anti-Semitic influence. We finally see the eventual takeover by Gentiles, which event was prophesied by Yeshua in the twin parable of the householder, beginning at Matthew 21:43. Beset by antagonism on either side—the Jewish high priest, Pharisees, Sanhedrin, etc., on the one hand and the Gentile leadership on the other—it is no wonder that the Lord's planting soon bore only wild grapes. He looked for judgment and righteousness but heard only the cry of oppression and the cry for deliverance from his people. Hence, the demise of the apostles signaled removal of the tower and winepress from the vineyard, and also the removal of the fence and hedge from around it.

The tower represents the watchman's vantage point, from whence surveillance of inside and outside activities can be monitored and supervised by spirit led men of God. Alluding to Genesis 22:14, where it is written, "Jehovah Jireh: In the mount of the Lord it shall be seen," we understand that removal of the tower meant transfer of oversight—that is, short- and long-term planning and daily execution in partnership with God—to the Church. Our partnership with God is affected through the Holy Spirit who was sent to indwell and work alongside us. He was meant to be our oversight as well.

The winepress is the processor that processes the fruit of the vine. In other words, the fruit of the vine are those who have been taught and reared up as disciples by the apostles. Again, this process cannot be carried out without the Holy Spirit who not only is the selector and teacher, but is also the one who stamps approval upon the disciple. This crucial process inside God's vineyard was terminated with the removal of the winepress. Antagonism from the Jewish secular and religious leaders coupled with anti-Semitism from the Gentile Church quenched the work of the Holy Spirit within the vineyard.

Finally, the fence and hedge about the vineyard protected it from intrusion and kept its sanctity intact. Removal of this protective barrier invited intrusions and eventual destruction of the vineyard as noted in the passage quoted from Isaiah 5.

But God is faithful; he will not suffer us to be tempted above what we are able to bear. So, just as he had begun preparing Shimshon to begin to deliver his people from under the yoke of the Philistines at the onset of the oppression, so did he begin to prepare the Church to minister his gospel of salvation to the whole world beginning with the house of Ya'akov immediately after he was glorified. This time, Satan the oppressor was given power to blindfold the eyes of national Israel to the spiritual realities of the kingdom. Therefore, it became the responsibility of the Church to lead Israel to the light that could lift the darkness away. While we know that Shimshon contended faithfully for Israel with great fervency, we cannot say the same for the Gentile Church which was given the mantle to represent God and his kingdom to the entire world beginning with Israel at Jerusalem.

Yes, the Church has had a disappointing performance relative to the Jews. In fact, many of the so-called Church fathers became so distraught at the hardheartedness of Jews to the gospel that they embarked upon a program of cursing and persecution of them. Justin Martyr accused the Jews of deicide or the murder of the son of God; Tertullian pronounced divine judgment upon them for crucifying Yeshua; Marcion taught that the Old Testament was superseded by the New Testament according to Matthew 5:17; Chrysostom taught that Jews are barbaric, going on to say, "I hate the Jews because they violate the law. I hate the synagogue because it has the law and the prophets. It is the duty of all Christians to hate the Jews." The teachings of Origen, who was labeled by two Church councils as a heretic, were used to develop the "New Israel of God" or replacement theology as known today; the Crusaders and Spanish Inquisition embarked upon ethnic cleansing of the Jews; Martin Luther, who at the start of his ministry declared the Jews to be a special people beloved of God, at the end of his ministry said, "God will see we are Christians when we get rid of the Jews. They are not heirs of the promises of God and deserve to die." Hitler said, "Martin Luther has been the greatest encouragement of my life. Luther was a great man. He was a giant ... He saw clearly that the Jews need to be destroyed, and we're only beginning to see that we need to carry this work on." By the way, Martin Luther died four days after preaching his last anti-Semitic message. As a testament to Luther's influence, Striker, the Nazi leader, at his trial in Nuremberg said, "I have never said anything that Martin Luther did not say."[57]

And this is just a sampling of the anti-Semitism displayed by the Church. Other anti-Semites include St. Augustine, and modern-day Reverend Jerry Falwell.[58] The Roman Catholic Church abolished worship on the Sabbath and instituted worship on Sunday (using the pagan worship day of the sun god), calling it the "Lord's Day."[59] In light of all this, would you, a custodian (Jew) of God's Word, relent and become as a pagan in order to be known as a Christian? Is it any wonder why Jews resisted, to the death if necessary at times, conversion to Christianity?

Naturally, a deep schism developed between Jews and those who called themselves Christians but still persecuted them. The few Jews who convert today refer to themselves as Messianic Jews, and they prefer to form separate congregations to worship, not desiring to become contaminated with observing pagan holidays and rituals, nor out-rightly rebelling against the Torah of God. As a result, not many Jews receive their Mashiach, and the Church, seemingly, could care less; not showering them with mercy, as is required. In response, the Lord repeatedly calls believers to enter into his vineyard. He asks, "Why are you idle all the day? Did I not command you to occupy till I return?" The current situation is that more Jews receive Yeshua at the hand of other Jewish believers than at the hand of Gentile believers. Why? Because Gentile believers have not paid heed to the Holy Spirit and the role he must play if the house of Ya'akov must be saved. For proof, just consider that there had been 1,800 years between the day of Pentecost and the Azusa Street Revival of 1906, which saw the Holy Spirit welcomed back into the Church. How else can there be an increase without him? Instead, the Church, without the Holy Spirit, has become as laborers without an overseer. Without the Holy Spirit, she labors in vain and the work can never be complete.

Many heathen nations have been given the task of chastising Israel as agents of God's wrath, and just as many have overstepped their mandates. They went overboard in punishing Israel (Assyria, Babylon, Philistia, etc.,) until the Lord said as it is written, "I am jealous for Jerusalem and for Zion with a great jealousy. And I am very sore displeased with the heathen that are at ease:

for I was but a little displeased, and they helped forward the affliction." But the Church is not heathenish, you say. Why then have we acted in a manner to dispossess Israel of her inheritance in the Lord? Therefore, thus saith the Lord, "I am returned to Jerusalem with mercies" (Zechariah 1:16).

What mercies? The very same love that the Church was mandated to love Israel with. For as ye in times past have not believed God, yet ye have now obtained mercy through their unbelief. Even so have these also now not believed that through your mercy they also may obtain mercy. Even though he hath said concerning his vineyard, "I will take away the hedge thereof, and it shall be eaten up; and break down the wall thereof, and it shall be trodden down: And I will lay it waste: it shall not be pruned nor digged; but there shall come up briers and thorns: I will also command the clouds that they rain no rain upon it." Yet he has great compassion for it. Why else would he return and hire laborers, not once, not twice, but repeatedly into his vineyard? Why else would he say, "Pray therefore the Lord of the harvest, that he will send forth laborers into his harvest?"

But the laborers have not proved worthy of their hire—neither clergy nor believer. For the clergy are those first hired into the vineyard, who worked full-time on the front line, bearing the full burdens associated with ministry and felt entitled to a greater reward than their fellows not employed full-time. They exalted themselves above the intents of the householder. The other laborers were content with their reward. However, knowing that work was available in the vineyard, not a single one ventured in, and none sought input from the steward. This, then, brings the work into question. First, was it completed? Next, how well was it done? For without the Lord, the laborer labors in vain. Finally, in view of the attitude of the laborers, the Lord says that he who will exalt himself will be abased, while he who does not seek to exalt himself will be exalted. In other words, he who would be great in heaven must put on the mind of servant-hood.

That you might know what is expected of you, the Church, he spake also this parable:

> A certain man had a fig tree planted in his vineyard: and he came and sought fruit thereon, and found none. Then said he unto the dresser of his vineyard, Behold, these three years I come seeking fruit on this fig tree, and find none: cut it down; why cumbereth it the ground? And he answering said unto him, Lord, let it alone this year also, till I shall dig about it, and dung it. And if it bear fruit, well: and if not, then after that thou shalt cut it down.
>
> Luke 13:6–9

Now he that hath ears to hear, let him understand; and he that hath eyes to see, let him perceive. The fig tree is Israel, and the dresser is the Gentile Church. According to this parable, we are required to intercede on Israel's behalf for the restoration of her sight and continue to enrich her with the fruit of the kingdom so that she too might blossom and bear good fruit. Many have presumed that the Church is supposed to make Israel jealous for her God by means of the immense material blessings that the Lord puts into its possession. Somehow, we have erroneously concluded that the lure of carnal riches will lead them to seek God. No, this is vanity. Where do we get the idea that carnality can engender spirituality? Does not Scripture tell us that the carnal mind is enmity with God? We are required to love Israel as we love ourselves.

This is the mercy that will peel away the scales with which the devil has blinded Israel.

Finally, take a look at the disposition of the Gentile Church toward Israel—very telling indeed! In answer to his master, the dresser says, "Allow me to tend the tree this one year and if it does not produce fruit then go ahead and cut it down." Notice the "time limited" compassion with which he pleads for mercy for the tree at the outset. Contrast that with the cold finality of his short patience, "If it bears fruit well and if it does not, then cut it down." Does not this mindset compare favorably with that of the husbandmen of Matthew 21:33–43 who said, "This is the heir; come, let us kill him, and let us seize on his inheritance?" Is this not the same route trod by the so-called Church fathers when they first began to tend the fig tree, and is this not their mandate that the Church still follows today? Now, compare his supposed compassion with the master's, who has borne patiently for three years.

Still, compare this lame intercession to that of a previous dresser for Israel. Exodus 32 relates an account of a similar pronouncement by the Master of the vineyard, "Now therefore let me alone, that my wrath may wax hot against them, and that I may consume them, and I will make of thee a great nation" (Exodus 32:10). The Gentile Church would have given its "eye-tooth" just to hear the Lord say something like this. If you don't believe this, tell me whence does "replacement theology" originate? But how did Moshe respond? With unfeigned love, he said, "Remember Abraham, Isaac, and Israel, thy servants, to whom thou swearest by thine own self, and saidst unto them, I will multiply your seed as the stars of heaven, and all this land that I have spoken of will I give unto your seed, and they shall inherit it for ever" (Exodus 32:13). Pertaining to this judgment, Moshe interceded on behalf of Israel four times. In his final intercession, Moshe, the sincere vinedresser, even offered up himself in place of Israel, saying, "Oh, this people have sinned a great sin, and have made them gods of gold. Yet now, if thou wilt forgive their sin; and if not, blot me, I pray thee, out of thy book which thou hast written" (Exodus 32:31–32). Can you imagine the Gentile Church ever laying its life down on behalf of Israel for any cause? Mercy!

But that is not the end of the matter, because the people of Israel, continuing in their sinful ways, provoked the Lord with an evil report concerning the promised land which they were poised to enter. Numbers 14:12 declares the Lord's hot anger toward his people at that time, "I will smite them with the pestilence, and disinherit them, and I will make of thee a greater nation and mightier than they." Once again, Moshe, the Lord's trusted vinedresser, would not remove himself from between the Lord and his people. Instead, he continued to stand in the gap for Israel until the Lord exchanged mercy for wrath toward his people when he said, "I have pardoned according to thy (Moshe's) word" (Numbers 14:20). Could not the Church have interceded or still intercede for the blindfold to be removed from Israel's eyes? Then the Lord would say, "I have removed the blindfold according to thy word." Wouldn't that be wonderful?

Parable of the Unmerciful Servant

Therefore is the kingdom of heaven likened unto a certain king, which would take account of his servants. And when he had begun to reckon, one was brought unto him, which owed him ten thousand talents. But forasmuch as he had not to pay, his lord commanded him to be sold, and his wife, and children, and all that he had, and payment to be made. The servant therefore fell down and worshiped him, saying, Lord, have patience with me, and I will pay thee all. Then the lord of that servant was moved with compassion, and loosed him, and forgave him the debt. But the same servant went out, and found one of his fellow servants, which owed him an hundred pence: and he laid hands on him, and took him by the throat, saying, Pay me that thou owest. And his fellow servant fell down at his feet, and besought him, saying, Have patience with me, and I will pay thee all. And he would not: but went and cast him into prison, till he should pay the debt. So when his fellow servants saw what was done, they were very sorry, and came and told unto their lord all that was done. Then his lord, after that he had called him, said unto him, O thou wicked servant, I forgave thee all that debt, because thou desiredst me: shouldest not thou also have had compassion on thy fellow servant, even as I had pity on thee? *And his lord was wroth, and delivered him to the tormentors, till he should pay all that was due unto him.* So likewise shall my heavenly Father do also unto you, if ye from your hearts forgive not every one his brother their trespasses.

Matthew 18:23–35

Now that we have received adequate warning from the Lord, it becomes our charge to take heed. As we read above, the king takes account of his servants whenever necessary. Is it possible that the Church has been reckoned and found wanting? Is that why she has never been able to do the "greater works," nor as yet receive at least thirtyfold from sowing into good soil? Or perhaps the Church has been turned over to the tormentors until she can be merciful to her fellow servant, Israel. What do you think? Make this a matter of prayer. Perhaps the

Lord is thundering to his Church, "Love your brethren as you love yourself!" Do you hear him?

Message Recap

Through the eyes of the world, man has come to accept that Shimshon was a great disappointment among the servants of God and a great throwback in the forward march of his work on earth. They see a man who committed one sin after another over a period of twenty years while in the service of the Lord, and who finally died as a result, before completing his mission.

Among those that matter, Christians and Jews have heaped undue condemnation upon this man over the years. Yet, they have failed to explain why God continued to operate through a disobedient, unrepentant, and unholy vessel. If that were not enough, the Church has heaped mound upon mound of condemnation and persecution on God's elect. Read the well-known anti-Semitic statement attributed to Bishop Cyprian, "Outside of the Church, there is no salvation."[60] Then hear what the revered St. Augustine wrote, "The true image of the Hebrew is Judas Iscariot, who sells the Lord for silver. The Jew can never understand the Scriptures and forever will bear the guilt for the death of Jesus."[61] Finally, Martin Luther urges Christians to "Set Jewish synagogues on fire for the honor of God."[62]

On one hand, we have both Christians and Jews condemning Shimshon, while on the other, we have Christians condemning and persecuting Jews. The common and unlikely factor in these ungodly acts is Christians—the body of Yeshua entrusted to share his love abroad. How did the Church wander so far away from its commission? This is what she was empowered to do,

but due to her "evil eye," she has conspired to dispossess
Israel of her inheritance in Yeshua. But this is an effort
in futility because Yeshua is Israel, God's firstborn. Yes,
the ministration of the kingdom of God was transferred
from Israel to the Church to produce fruit thereof, not
to exclude Israel there-from. The apostle Shaul asks, "If
their temporary fall results in riches to the Gentiles, can
you imagine the impact of the fullness of their inclusion
in the Church?" The Church must repudiate the vitriolic,
false teachings of all so-called Church fathers and the
Roman Catholic Church and repent before God. We
must pray that the Lord will rid us of our "evil eye" and
humble ourselves under the leading of the Holy Spirit so
that we might fulfill our commission. Amen?

If the Church could peer through the eyes of God
at Shimshon, it would see a man, fully commissioned to
do exactly what he did—not only to begin to deliver his
people, Israel, but also to portray the ways of God with
his elect. For the blessing of Shimshon (Psalm 32:1–2)
has been held in store for Israel until Yeshua returns.

At that time, he shall forgive Ya'akov's iniquity and
will not remember his sins again. It will be just like when
Shimshon despaired of life and died in a figure. Then on
the eighth day, his head was divinely consecrated again
unto God. The parallel with Israel is this: When the
nations are gathered against national Israel, then will she
despair and call upon the name of the Lord. And though
they had not believed, still through his mercies he shall
appear and save Israel. Marana Tha. Amen!

EPILOGUE

The Finished Work

The work that Shimshon began, to open the door of salvation, was completed in Yeshua ha Mashiach upon the cross, symbolized with the veil of the temple being rent in two. Since then, the throne of mercy and grace is accessible unto all men through Yeshua, so that none should perish.

Unfortunately, too many perish because they do not and cannot differentiate between the doorway that is Yeshua unto eternal life and the broad path that leads to destruction. The doorway to eternal life is perpetually lit up brighter than a thousand suns, whereas the pathway of destruction is perpetually cloaked in the blackness of a million nights. Therefore, it is beyond reason that myriad souls should successfully navigate the pathway to destruction in darkness than the scant numbers that enter through the brightly lit doorway to eternal life.

The root of such an unlikely scenario is due to the similarity between spiritual darkness and light in our generation. Though darkness cannot comprehend light, it is the light that has muted itself in darkness. Therefore, the world cannot discern between the near sameness of the two.

Even as the wilderness Church was warned not to intermarry with the heathens in the promised land because, said God, "They will turn your sons away from following after me," so has he warned the present-day Church not to be conformed to the world, but to be transformed by the renewing of our minds daily. This—our disobedience—has blurred the distinction between the Gentile Church and the world.

Yeshua, the light of the world, is also the light that resides in every individual member of the Church. He is the light that never dims or loses brightness. Therefore, the Church, singly and collectively, as the vessel containing light, must light up the path that leads to the doorway of eternal life. Hence, the Church has done a great disservice to the world. First, by removing from its exalted place atop the hill and concealing itself, the world cannot find the doorway to salvation. In other words, the Church—the light that beckoned atop the hill—has removed to the valley below and covered itself.

This disservice is directly opposed to the will of God and his purpose for the predominantly Gentile Church today. The Church is too quick to point out the faults and shortcomings of the children of Israel, never realizing that it has fallen far short of provoking the Jew to jealousy. Instead, Jews have been and are being provoked to turn away from their Savior in droves. Still, this turning away is according to the foreknowledge of God from before the foundation of the world and shall not be to the eternal hurt of the Jew.

There is a purpose for the spiritual blindness of the Jews, even as there is for the salvation of Gentiles. In Romans 11:11, the apostle Shaul (Paul) asks: "Have they stumbled that they should fall? God forbid: but rather through their fall salvation is come unto the Gentiles for to provoke them to jealousy." Now, in harmony with his master plan, this blinding of the Jews lasts only until the full number of Gentiles have entered the kingdom of heaven. After that, he removes all of their ungodliness so that all Israel shall be saved, "For I would not, brethren, that ye should be ignorant of this mystery, lest ye should be wise in your own conceits; that blindness in part is happened to Israel, until the fullness of the Gentiles be come in. And so all Israel shall be saved... There shall come out of Sion the Deliverer, and shall turn away ungodliness from Ya'akov: For this is my covenant with them, when I shall take away their sins" (Romans 11:25–27).

Through unbelief of the elect, God's mercy was extended to the Gentiles so that a people who did not know God, neither believed, might obtain salvation. In turn, God desires and expects that the Gentiles will extend this same mercy to Israel so that they might obtain mercy to believe. Shaul (Paul) puts it this way, "For as ye in times past have not believed God, yet have now obtained mercy through their unbelief: Even so have these also now not believed, that through your mercy they also may obtain mercy" (Romans 11:30–31).

Through Shaul, God adds the final clincher. Despite the shortcoming of the Gentile Church to fulfill the Great Commission to the Jew first and then to the world, God declares, "All Israel shall be saved!" How? "For God hath concluded them all in unbelief, that he might have mercy upon all" (Romans 11:32). In other words, God has leveled the playing field whereby all of mankind might be saved.

If Shimshon's work began to deliver Israel, then Yeshua's completion of that work provides continuance of deliverance to the Jew even as it extends the same deliverance to Gentiles also. Shaul concludes, "O the depth of the riches both of the wisdom and knowledge of God! How unsearchable are his judgments, and his ways past finding out" (Romans 11:33). Glory be to Yeshua ha Mashiach, (the substance of Shimshon, the wedge that began to pry open the door of salvation to the Jew first), who finally opened that door fully to all mankind. Amen!

BIBLIOGRAPHY

1. Dake's Annotated Reference Bible. The Holy Bible: King James Version. Finis Jennings Dake, 33rd ed. Lawrenceville: Dake Bible Sales, 2005.
2. Halley's Bible Handbook with the NIV, 25th ed. James E. Ruarck (ed.), Grand Rapids: Zondervan, 2000.
3. Ravenhill, Leonard. Why Revival Tarries. 33rd ed. Minneapolis: Bethany House, 1988.
4. BBC News/Health. Samson Was Mentally Ill. Dr. Eric Altschuler. 2001. http://www.news.bbc.co.uk/2/hi/health/1170519.stm
5. JewishEncyclopedia.com. Samson. Joseph Jacobs, Ira M. Price, Wilhelm Bacher, Jacob Z. Lauterbach. 2006. http://www.jewishencyclopedia.com/
6. Josephus, Flavius. The Works of Josephus: Complete and Unabridged. Translated by William Whiston, a.m. 4th printing, Peabody: Hendrickson, 1989.

7. Therefinersfire.org. Anti-Semitism and the Early Church Fathers. *Christian Hatred and Persecution of the Jews.* Phyllis Petty. http://www.therefinersfire.org/antisemitism_in_church .htm

8. Reluctant-messenger.com. The Complete Canons of the Synod of Laodicea. The Council of Laodicea in Phrygia Pacatiana 364 AD. http://www.reluctant-messenger.com/council-of-laodicea.htm

9. Sullivan-county.com. Lewis Loflin (ed.), Christian Jew-Haters. 2007. http://www.sullivan-county.com/identity /jew_haters.htm

10. Jewish New Testament. Translated by David H. Stern. Jerusalem: Jewish New Testament Publications, 1989.

English-Hebraic
Glossary of Names

Aaron—Aharon
Abraham—Avraham
Christ/Messiah—Mashiach
David—David
Esau—Esav
Holy Spirit, the—Ruach-Ha-Kodesh
Isaac—Yitzchak
Isaiah—Yesha'yahu
Israel—Israel
Jacob, James—Ya'akov
Jeremiah—Yirmeyahu
Jesus—Yeshua
John—Yochanan
Joseph—Yosef
Joshua—Y'hoshua
Judah/Judea—Y'hudah
Mary/Miriam—Miryam
Matthew—Mattityahu
Moses—Moshe

Paul—Shaul
Peter—Kefa
Rachel—Rachel
Rebekah—Rivkah
Ruth—Rut
Samson—Shimshon
Samuel—Shmu'el
Sarah—Sarah
Zechariah—Z'kharyeh

ENDNOTES

Preface

1   Ravenhill, Leonard. Why Revival Tarries, P.18.
     Minneapolis: Bethany House, 1988. 2

Chapter 1

2   Numbers: 2–8
3   Hebrews 11:32
4   Halley's Bible Handbook with the NIV.
     Samson, P. 207. James E. Ruarck (ed.),
     Grand Rapids: Zondervan 2000.
5   The Works of Josephus: Complete and
     Unabridged. Antiquities of the Jews, Book 5,
     Chapter 8. Translated by William Whiston,
     a.m. Peabody: Hendrickson, 1989.
6   The Jeweish Encyclopedia. Samson.
     2002, JewishEncyclopedia.com.
7   BBC News Report. Samson 'was mentally ill.'
     Dr. Eric Altschuler. BBC News, Thursday, 15
     February 2001.

Chapter 2

 8 Judges 2:1–23
 9 Judges 13:1–16:31

Chapter 3

 10 Genesis 15:2; 17:16
 11 Genesis 25:21
 12 Genesis 30:1, 2, 22
 13 1 Samuel 1:11
 14 Luke 1:15
 15 Judges 13:5
 16 Judges 13:7
 17 Leviticus 21:1–8; Acts 21:24
 18 Psalm 138:26
 19 Numbers 23:19
 20 Hebrews 6:12

Chapter 4

 21 Judges 1:10–2:19
 22 2 Kings 13:17
 23 John 1:12
 24 Romans 9:21
 25 Psalm 82:1
 26 Genesis 49:16

Chapter 5

 27 Leviticus 27:1–9
 28 Judges 13:19
 29 Judges 13:15, 17
 30 Mark 1:12
 31 Judges 3:5–6
 32 2 Samuel 3:18

33 Matthew 1:21; 18:11
34 The Works of Josephus: Complete and
    Unabridged. Antiquities of the Jews, Book,
    Chapter 8. Translated by William Whiston,
    a.m. Peabody: Hendrickson, 1989.
35 Judges 16:3
36 Colossians 2:15
37 Psalm 103:12
38 Micah 7:19
39 Numbers 6:9–12
40 1 John 1:9
41 Jeremiah 1:5

Chapter 6
42 Jeremiah 1:5
43 Judges 13:5

Chapter 7
44 Hebrews 12:29

Chapter 8
45 Isaiah 5:20; 2 Timothy 3:1–12

Chapter 9
46 Amos 1:8
47 Romans 11:29
48 Proverbs 15:29
49 Romans 3:25
50 Romans 11:12
51 Zechariah 12:2–3
52 Romans 11:26
53 Zechariah 12:10; 13:1, 6
54 Jeremiah 31:13, 31–34
55 Romans 3:30; Galatians 3:8

56 Psalm 114:1–2
57 Anti-Semitism And The Early Church Fathers;
   http://www.therefinersfire.org/antisemitism
58 Christian Jew-Haters; http://www.sullivan_
   county.com/identity/jew_haters.htm
59 Council of Laodicea; http://www.
   reluctant-messenger.com/
60 Christian Jew-Haters; http://www.sullivan_
   county.com/identity/jew_haters.htm
61 Ibid
62 Ibid

e|LIVE

listen|imagine|view|experience

AUDIO BOOK DOWNLOAD INCLUDED WITH THIS BOOK!

In your hands you hold a complete digital entertainment package. In addition to the paper version, you receive a free download of the audio version of this book. Simply use the code listed below when visiting our website. Once downloaded to your computer, you can listen to the book through your computer's speakers, burn it to an audio CD or save the file to your portable music device (such as Apple's popular iPod) and listen on the go!

How to get your free audio book digital download:

1. Visit www.tatepublishing.com and click on the e|LIVE logo on the home page.
2. Enter the following coupon code:
   0728-6b0b-ed54-b18e-00ba-8aa7-b5c7-484d
3. Download the audio book from your e|LIVE digital locker and begin enjoying your new digital entertainment package today!

Printed in Great Britain
by Amazon